"There are a lot of book marketing 'experts' out there, most of whom have never actually done the things they're pretending to be experts about. Joanna Penn really has made her mark in indie publishing and How to Market a Book is worth reading for anyone looking to do the same."

Ryan Holiday, Bestselling author of
The Obstacle is the Way and *Perennial Seller: The Art of Making and Marketing Work That Lasts*

"Joanna is not just a go-to-expert for writers, she's a go-to-expert for the experts like myself. She's been working continuously as an author and entrepreneur for more than a decade, and has connections and conversations with people across the publishing industry that put her insights and advice into a class of their own."

Jane Friedman, Author, Publishing Consultant, Speaker

"I read the first edition of How To Market A Book shortly after it was published in 2014. Until then marketing was a dark, terrifying frontier. This book changed the way I approached marketing, because it removed the fear of getting started. The 2017 edition is more of the same, but updated to match the new indie landscape. The chapter on Sampling is worth pressing that buy button all by itself, but there are plenty of other great nuggets too.

One of the most important is author branding, something Joanna Penn has mastered. How do we know that? If you're a fan of the podcast *you will literally hear this book in Joanna's voice as your read it.* Now that's branding.

Chris Fox, Bestselling author of
Write to Market and Six Figure Author

"Joanna Penn has an intuitive understanding of how marketing works and how that pertains to the unique challenge of reaching readers and selling books. Her advice is always practical, actionable, and - most importantly of all - effective."

David Gaughran, author,
Let's Get Digital and *Let's Get Visible*

"There are thousands of books about how to sell books but this is one of the few written by someone who walks the talk. A bestselling author herself, who has shared every step of her publishing journey with empathy and generosity, Penn is an inspiration to multitudes of writers. Whether you're an indie, trade published or hybrid author, whether you are just starting out or have already sold widely, whether you love marketing or hate it, you will learn from this book."

Orna Ross, Author and Director,
Alliance of Independent Authors

"Joanna Penn's wonderful podcast was a major influence on me when I was a struggling author, trying to work out how to get readers to discover my first self-published books. Her non-fiction, too, has been a life-saver, and this revised edition of How to Market a Book is filled with her hallmarks: a thorough approach, comprehensive scope and a delivery that is patient and easy to read in a way that is 100% "Joanna." I commend it to new authors, but also to experienced veterans who would benefit from a review of their marketing to ensure that they are up to date with the most current thinking."

Mark Dawson, bestselling thriller author
and creator of the Advertising for Authors course
and the Self-Publishing Formula podcast

"The Third Edition of Joanna Penn's *How to Marketing a Book* does not disappoint! Book marketing changes fast, and with this updated content Joanna solidifies this book's place as one of the must-read books on every author's bookshelf."

Jim Kukral, BusinessAroundABook.com
and the Sell More Books Show podcast

"Joanna Penn's How to Market a Book is the most up to date, personable guide to modern book marketing I know. Packed with tips from the charming and well-informed Penn, it's an essential guide for indie authors who want to keep up with the ever-shifting world of book marketing."

Joel Friedlander, author and founder of
TheBookDesigner.com

"Joanna Penn's How to Market a Book is a solid reference guide for beginners and experienced authors alike. The book provides straightforward, actionable advice you can use from day one. This book is a must-have in any author's library."

Honoree Corder, Author, *The Prosperous Writer*
book series and *You Must Write a Book*

"Right now, self-publishing is a wide open opportunity for writers. But it's a confusing and increasingly competitive field. Joanna Penn is one of the guides I rely on to help me navigate the maze, make better marketing decisions, and sell more books. If you read this book, she'll do the same for you."

Mark McGuinness, Poet, Coach and author of
Productivity for Creative People and Resilience: Facing Down Rejection and *Criticism on the Road to Success*

"Puzzled by marketing? Save years of research and trial and error with Penn's spot-on modern classic."

Bryan Cohen, author of *How to Write a Sizzling Synopsis* and co-host of the Sell More Books Show podcast

How to
Market
a
BOOK

For Authors by an Author

Third Edition

Joanna Penn

How To Market A Book Third Edition (2017)

Copyright © 2017, 2021 by Joanna Penn

First Edition published 2013. Second Edition published 2014.
Third Edition published 2017, updated 2021.

ISBN: 978-1-912105-87-8

Published by Curl Up Press

Requests to publish work from this book should be sent to:
joanna@CurlUpPress.com

Cover and Interior Design: JD Smith

Printed by KDP Print

www.CurlUpPress.com

Contents

Part 5: Marketing Strategy and Book Launches **261**

Dedicated to my readers and community at
The Creative Penn and the listeners to my podcast.
Thank you for making my creative life possible!

Introduction

Writing for the sake of writing is absolutely brilliant, but many of us have ambitions to see our books in the hands (and devices) of millions. We publish to be read, otherwise our words would remain in private journals. We want our words to touch people's minds and change their lives, even for a short while. And perhaps we'd like to make some money doing creative work we love.

But even if your book is truly outstanding, there are millions of books for readers to choose from and more being published every day. Plus, there are increasing numbers of TV shows, movies and games, as well as addictive social media clickbait.

There is increasing competition for people's attention, so how will your book stand out?

Authors are often responsible for marketing their books, however they choose to publish. But marketing isn't a skill that most authors have, and there is little formal training. So when your book hits the shelves, and the sales *don't* start rolling in, there's only one thing to do. Keep writing more books and get to grips with marketing.

This guide is **for authors who want to sell more books**, both for traditionally published authors who want to take control of their future, and for self-published authors who want to jumpstart a career.

It's also about going **beyond the book** because the methods in this guide can take you from being an author into professional speaking, making money from other products and creating opportunities that you can't even imagine yet.

There are **short-term tactics** for those who want to spike immediate sales, but the focus is more about instilling values and marketing principles that will help your **long-term career as a writer**. Because, despite the new tools that arrive every month, **the fundamentals of marketing don't change**.

When I look back at my marketing journey, it has mostly been a repetition of things that I enjoy doing – blogging, podcasting, Twitter – and the attitudes of generosity and social karma. The tools you choose might be different to mine, but **what really matters is consistency and incorporating marketing into your daily author life**. In that way, you will build a readership and become part of a community over time.

There are no rules in this game, but learning authentic marketing has certainly changed my life, so read on, and I'll share everything I know with you.

What has changed in this updated Third Edition?

When I first started self-publishing and book marketing nearly ten years ago, being an indie author was still a fringe activity, considered second-best to traditional publishing. That attitude has almost completely gone away now, and the bestseller charts are filled with self-published books.

Back then, the main marketing activities were still around traditional media, and it was hard to get traction unless you had an established author platform. But the rise in the number of authors now self-publishing has led to new tools and opportunities, and a whole industry has grown up offering services to those who need help.

The publishing platforms have also matured, offering benefits like pre-orders and paid advertising that had previously only been available to bigger publishers. There are authors building platforms for the long term, using blogs and podcasts to grow an audience, but there are also authors who use production speed to hack the algorithms, and combine paid ads with email list building and big data analytics.

There are more options than ever, and more voices offering advice. It can be overwhelming, so I hope that the principles in this edition will help you decide what works best for you and your author career.

This book is structured into parts and can be read in order, or you can dip into the chapter that you are most interested in straight away.

Part 1. Marketing Principles

This section gives you an insight into some of the fundamental concepts that you need to understand before you jump into specific tactics. These are the precursors to the actual marketing activity, the mindset and the polarities of marketing. The decisions you make here will help guide your marketing plans.

Part 2. Your Book Fundamentals

People find your book in two ways, either through the book itself or through you, the author. This section goes into how to optimize your book so that it can be discovered more easily on the book sales websites. If you *only* do the things covered here, you will be streets ahead of many other authors, and if you leap into more advanced options without getting this right, you might be wasting your time.

Part 3. No Platform Needed: Short-term Marketing

You don't need a blog or a podcast or a website or an email list to sell books. This section will help you to get your book sales moving through paid advertising, production speed and other methods. You can implement these ideas without an author platform or alongside one for spike marketing, plus they can be especially useful for authors writing under pseudonyms.

Part 4. Your Author Platform: Long-term Marketing

This section focuses on what you need to have in place for a career as an author as well as some ideas for building your author platform. It includes author branding, your website and email list, content marketing, social media, audio, video, PR, professional speaking and more.

Part 5: Marketing Strategy and Book Launches

Strategy is about choosing what you do, as well as what you *don't* do. You can't implement everything in this book, so you need to create a strategy for how you will incorporate the various aspects into a plan for your book. It might also be different per author brand, and I share how I market each of my three author names in this section, along with looking at how to relaunch backlist books and questions to consider if your book isn't selling.

What about marketing fiction vs. non-fiction books?

There are some techniques that would be better for one rather than the other. I mention within each chapter when these distinctions become relevant, but in general, you should consider everything in this guide as a possibility for your marketing efforts.

Don't get overwhelmed!

Just start with one thing and see how it works for a specific length of time, rather than attempting everything at once with a scattergun approach. You can certainly spend all your time marketing when you should probably be writing the next book.

This is also not an exhaustive list of marketing options. It is just my take on a vast subject based on my experience, so I have included links to more resources within the text for you to take your study further if you want to. There will always be new and shiny tools to play with, but I have focused on the principles and fundamentals to help you navigate into the future.

In each section, consider how you want to use the information. Do you want or need to put it into practice and how might that impact your book sales both now and later in your career?

Happy marketing!

* * *

Please note: This book contains some affiliate links to products/services I recommend and use myself.

My story

This guide is written from my perspective as an author of fiction and non-fiction, as well as a professional speaker and entrepreneur. It contains everything I've learned on the journey, in the hope that you will save time, effort and heartache on your own path. I'll start by explaining my background, so you understand that you're not alone.

I started out seriously writing in 2006 and first self-published the book of my heart in 2008 about how to change your life and your career by finding a job you love (rewritten and released in 2012 as *Career Change*).

Back then, the Kindle was brand new, and ebooks weren't mainstream. Self-publishing still had the stigma of being a last-resort option, a far cry from the positive choice it has become for many today. But I was determined to change people's lives, so I paid for a print run of two thousand books. They arrived in boxes and sat in my garage as I tried to work out how to shift them into the hands of readers.

Within a few weeks, I discovered that selling books was a completely different skill-set and that the journey of writing and publishing the book was only the beginning. The boxes began to take on a sinister look, mocking my inability to sell them.

I had no background in sales or marketing, and although I was working as a business consultant at the time, implementing Accounts Payable systems was no training for book sales. Plus, I have a degree in Theology from Oxford University, hardly a useful specialism for selling books!

So I started to learn about marketing, reading everything I could on the subject, taking online classes, buying audio courses and immersing myself in this new world. I discovered direct marketing and copywriting, then investigated traditional media, appearing on national TV, radio and in newspapers.

When this didn't shift my sales significantly, I started to learn about online marketing as well as using ebooks and print-on-demand to publish more effectively. I was living in Australia at that point, a tiny book market, and I wanted to reach readers in the US and UK, so the Internet was really the only way.

I initially thought 'sales and marketing' were scammy and slimy, and of course, there is a nasty side if people choose to follow it, but I quickly found that it wasn't the only option.

There was another way to market that involved offering **useful content, building a treasured brand, giving value to people and being authentic.**

So I learned about using blogging, social media, podcasting and video to connect with people worldwide. These methods of marketing felt right to me, because one of my motivations for writing a self-help book was to help people, and this was just another way. I immersed myself in learning about online marketing, focusing on the principle of attracting attention by being useful. It gels with the way I want to live my life and also markets my books and my business at the same time.

I started TheCreativePenn.com in 2008, as my third blog attempt, and it became more of a way to catalog everything I was learning. I was working full-time as a business consultant at the time, spending my days in cubicle misery. At that point, I had no traffic to my new website, no one knew who I was, I only had one non-fiction book to my name, and it had sold about 100 copies. I had no online platform – no email list, no podcast, no video, no social networks. I didn't know any authors, and I had no way to connect with anyone.

But I put what I learned into action. Writing and marketing every day.

And over time, things changed.

In 2011, I was able to quit my day job and go full-time as an author-entrepreneur. I cover that in much more detail in my book, *How to Make a Living with your Writing*. In 2015, my husband was able to quit his corporate job to join me working in the business, and we now make a multi-six-figure income.

As I write this updated version, I have 16 novels and eight non-fiction books. My books have sold over 500,000 copies in 83 countries and I am a New York Times and USA Today bestseller. My website TheCreativePenn.com has been voted one of the top blogs for writers several years running, and I'm an award-winning creative entrepreneur and international professional speaker.

None of this would have been possible without learning how to market my books.

But only a few years ago, I had nothing. It just takes time and consistent effort to grow. So, it's all possible, and I hope this book helps you with your own author journey.

PART 1: Marketing Principles

1.1 The marketing mindset

Ask most authors about book marketing and they will roll their eyes. Let's face it, we are authors because we love to write, most often alone in our rooms or inside our heads in a caf⊠. We want someone else to handle the marketing. But times have changed, and at some point, you will have to get involved. Marketing will be a lot easier and more fun if you start by changing your mindset. Here are some ways to reframe book marketing so you can read the rest of this book with a new perspective.

Marketing is sharing what you love with people who will appreciate hearing about it.

Marketing doesn't have to be scammy or sucky, or forcibly ramming your book down people's throats in real life or on social media.

Perhaps you're writing a book about how you recovered from Type 2 diabetes. Don't you think people want to hear about that? Or you've written a kick-ass action-adventure thriller that will blow the socks off those miserable commuters you share a train carriage with and help them to escape the grind for a few hours. Don't you think they want to know about it?

You've got to find ways to connect with people who would want your book if they heard about it – that's marketing these days. It is not scammy or sucky or awful (if you don't want it to be). It's about authenticity and the principles around 'know, like and trust' as well as the technical things that you'll find out about in this guide.

You also need to reframe marketing because we are ALL salespeople these days. In Daniel Pink's book *To Sell Is Human* he explains how the world has changed, and how the job of 'salesman' doesn't really exist anymore, but that we're all involved in selling every day. It might be 'selling' healthy food to your kids, or 'selling' yourself to advance your career, or as authors, it's pitching our ideas to agents and publishers or trying to get people to be interested in us and our books.

If you change your attitude, it will all be a lot easier!

You are responsible for your success. You need to do marketing however you choose to publish.

Many first-time authors assume that a publisher will do all the marketing for them, but authors always have to get involved. If you're traditionally published, it often involves physical appearances at bookstore signings, literary festivals or conventions, as well as media appearances and reader correspondence. Some authors have publicists within the publishing house or an external marketing firm organizing things for them, but often only for the launch period, and that won't pay the bills for your long-term writing career. Of course, if you do get a publicist and you do get media attention, you are the one who has to speak at events and festivals, do media interviews and more.

Publishers will sort out distribution and work with bookstore buyers, as well as advising on what you can do to help them market the book. You'll likely have to do all the platform stuff we cover in Part 4 anyway. So even though you might have a team to advise over the launch period, you will still need to do a lot yourself. And after the initial launch phase, you will likely be left alone as the publisher moves onto the next author and book on the publishing schedule. As Pulitzer Prize winning author, David Mamet said when he announced his decision to self-publish, "publishing is like Hollywood – nobody ever does the marketing they promise."

On the flip-side, authors new to self-publishing assume that they will sell books purely because they loaded their book up on Amazon. But they swiftly find out that's not enough to get noticed among the hundreds of thousands of new books added every year.

So remember, you are responsible for your author career. No one else cares as much about your book as you do. If you empower yourself with knowledge around marketing and put it into action, you will always be able to sell your own books and make an income from writing.

Marketing is creative, and your writing can be marketing in itself

"Good marketers tell a story."

Seth Godin

If you reframe marketing as creative and fun, you will find yourself enjoying it more. There are a lot of creative ways to market, you just have to find what works for you. For example, I love taking pictures and share a lot of images on Twitter, Instagram, Pinterest and on my Facebook pages. I'm taking pictures on my smart phone anyway, and it only takes a minute to share them online. It provides a glimpse of my life, and if the picture resonates with you, perhaps you'll follow me and eventually be interested enough to read one of my books.

You can also use writing as your main marketing mechanism. Write short stories, flash fiction or articles and share them on your blog, or publish one article or story a week on Amazon to keep the algorithms pumping. You could post your work in progress on Wattpad or other story-sharing sites.

Think about your own social and reading behavior and then consider how you could incorporate that into your book marketing because the best marketing comes from empathy with the reader. Since you are likely an avid reader in the genre you write in, you know how your readers behave. Switch your mindset from the author to the customer viewpoint. What makes you stop scrolling to read or watch? What do you do with that spare minute in the supermarket queue? How could you reach a reader like you?

It's all about learning

I have no formal qualifications in writing, publishing, marketing or running a business. I've learned everything over the years from books, audio, online courses and live events. I'm still learning from new books, Facebook groups and a lot of podcasts across multiple niches because marketing changes over time.

If you love learning new things, then book marketing becomes something else to discover. There's no need to be afraid. No one is going to die if you screw up an interview or run a Facebook Ad that doesn't work, or if you need to change your cover to something more genre-specific. We all make mistakes and learn from them. If you hear about something new, research it and try it out. If it works and you enjoy it, carry on. If it doesn't work, learn more and maybe try again.

In 2008, I started three different blogs. The Creative Penn was my third and the only one that I couldn't stop writing for. I still schedule content months in advance because I share what I learn and I never stop learning. I'm a super geek!

In 2009, I discovered Twitter. I was petrified of it, but put up a profile and gave it go. It remains my favorite platform for connection and marketing. I also tried podcasting in 2009 and loved that. Other things have fallen by the way-side. For example, I am never going to do much Live video because it's just not me. But you don't know until you try.

The tools and tactics mentioned in this guide will change over time, as will you and your priorities for writing and selling books. The most important thing to focus on is an attitude of play, experimentation and learning. We can gather all kinds of ideas from other people, but in the end, we have to make our own decisions about what works for our books and our lives.

In this book, I offer you a smorgasbord of options, but don't do everything at once and try different options over time. You can also revisit older ideas as tactics change. For example, I had stopped using content marketing on my fiction site, JFPenn.com, because it wasn't having any impact on my book sales. But then Facebook Advertising came along, and I installed a pixel on the site and now it's worth using content marketing to attract my target audience because I can re-target them with advertising for my books. There's more on this type of paid advertising in Part 3.

A case study is not evidence. Experiment and measure.

There's an old saying: "50% of marketing works, but no one knows which 50%." If you do everything in this book, you will have so many entry-points into your book ecosystem that it will become hard to track what works. It's also hard to track the effectiveness of some types of marketing. For example, if I appear on a podcast interview, someone might listen to that six months later and then buy my book, and I will never know how they found it.

But there are also a lot of techniques that can be attributed to specific marketing campaigns. For example, paid ads on sites like BookBub can provide an obvious spike in sales and you can also use tracking links like bitly and other services to see where sales originate.

Of course, your ability to do prompt and specific sales tracking will depend on your level of control over the book. Self-published ebooks are the easiest to measure, as you can log into the author sales portals and see how many books have sold on a specific day. If you are doing a promotion, you can see within hours how that impacts on sales and ranking. Traditionally published authors can look at sales rank as an approximation for the effectiveness of marketing activities.

You can also find out what other people are doing. One of the amazing things about being an author these days is how many writers are sharing their experiences online, whereas it used to be a very closed environment with a lot of smoke and mirrors. Now authors are collaborating and helping each other. There are even some Facebook groups and blogs where authors share their marketing experiences as well as results and actual data.

Read these and get ideas and try them yourself but remember, it might not work for your genre or your price point or your country, or any number of other variables. A case study is not evidence.

You can only try things and then note down what works

for you in each situation, so that you can improve on it next time. Take screen-prints of your rankings and put your sales into a spreadsheet or document along with the techniques you used because, believe me, you'll forget what you did a few months later!

You can hire other people to do marketing for you

There are plenty of freelancers, virtual assistants and companies who will market your book for you. But the truth is that you know your book better than anyone. You also know *you* better than anyone, and it takes trial and error to figure out what kind of marketing works best for each person and each book. For example, you might hire a publicist to get you on TV and in the papers only to find that you hate doing traditional media, but you'd rather post photos on Instagram instead. Or you might hire someone to do your Facebook advertising only to discover that you prefer networking in person or speaking in public. You might end up paying a lot of money for little results, so it's good to at least understand what you want before you start outsourcing.

I did everything myself for the first few years. Now I have one person who does the audio for my podcast, another who does the video for YouTube, another who does the transcription of the show notes, another one who edits and formats the show notes. I have people who write articles and a virtual assistant who formats and schedules them, as well as someone who helps run and analyze my paid ads. All these freelance assistants do smaller pieces of work, but I understand it all and could do it again if I wanted to.

To be clear, I only started to hire people once my author income justified it, and now I'm thrilled to have a great team. But I recommend you start by doing things yourself and outsource over time.

If you do want help with book marketing, check out the curated professionals at Reedsy, which you can find at www.TheCreativePenn.com/reedsy

Marketing is more than a book launch

There is a pervasive myth in publishing that the launch is everything and that one big push will rocket your book up the charts and you'll be a multi-millionaire. Yippee! This might be because it occasionally happens for an author, but it's more of a rare lightning strike. Most authors sell books over the long term, and as you write more books, a launch becomes a regular event.

The short-term spike launch approach comes from traditional publishing and print books. Publishers and booksellers have monthly business cycles, and each book gets a short window of opportunity to make an impact before everyone moves on to the next set of books in the queue. There is limited shelf space in physical stores, and those front tables cost money!

But the world of book buying has changed, and now it's more about the long tail, where there are fewer blockbusters but many more authors making a decent living in the margins of the industry.

So, the launch doesn't have to be everything for us. In fact, initial launch period sales are often disappointing compared to what happens once the algorithms kick in and you get some traction around reviews and reputation. In August 2016, a boxset of the first three books in my ARKANE thriller series hit the USA Today bestseller list. Those books were originally published in 2011-2012, but they were brand new to the readers who found them and my sales were certainly better that week than they had been on first publication.

If you want to be an author for the long term, then consider a business model based on long term sales for your lifetime as an author, not on an unsustainable spike on launch. It's certainly good to plan for a successful launch, as covered in Part 5, but you're also building a foundation for the long-term, which means incorporating ways to keep marketing your books even when you're not in the launch phase.

Marketing is an investment. You need a budget.

All publishers have a budget for book marketing. How much they spend will be different per book and per author, based on how many copies they expect to sell. Clearly, Stephen King will get more marketing budget than an un-known author on their third book in a low-selling series. But the point is that some money is set aside to push the book in front of readers. If you want your book to have any chance of reaching your target market, then you will need a budget.

Marketing is an investment, which means you will need to put in the time and/or money now, with the expectation that you will receive money later to offset those costs. All businesses invest in marketing to drive sales. If you want to sell books, you need to do the same.

How much you spend is, of course, up to you. Many au-thors spend far more time than money, and that's what I did when I first started out. After setting up a website, I used content marketing and social media to attract atten-tion to my books. I only used paid advertising once I was making money. These days, I have a marketing budget set aside, but you can certainly use most of the options in this book by using your time.

Decide on your definition of success

A lot of authors say that they want to 'sell more books,' that they want to be a 'successful' author or that they want 'everybody' to read their book. But those goals are too broad, and it will be difficult to know when you have succeeded or hit your target unless you clearly define what you mean.

You need to consider what your definition of success is, and what your goals are, because this will help you to shape what you do with your time, money and effort. You also need a wider perspective on the 'why' behind what you are doing, because only that will carry you through the inevitable difficult times.

For example, if you want to hit the New York Times list or to make number one in romance or any big category, you need to have a large email list of people waiting for your book or pay for spike promotion. If you want your book on the shelves of your local bookstore, it's possible to do this as an indie author publishing through Ingram Spark, and then by fostering relationships with local booksellers. If you want to make a consistent level of income every month, then you'll focus marketing efforts on list-building over time, growing a base of happy customers ready to buy books or building a business beyond the book.

Your definition of success and your goals for this book and your author career will shape how you approach your publishing choices and marketing efforts. Always try to be specific with your goals and what you consider success to be, and you are more likely to make it happen.

So, what's your definition of success?

Be very specific around your book and also your career as an author over the next few years. Break that down into steps as you go through this book. For example, if you want to sell 10,000 books, how will you start by selling the first ten in the first month?

What type of marketing suits your personality?

You might not believe this if you've seen me at live events, but I'm an introvert and like to spend a lot of time on my own. Hey, I'm a writer! Chances are you're similar in many ways. I'm not shy, but I need quiet and silence and time alone to recharge. So going to live networking events with crowds of people isn't really me, but social networking online at times I can pick and choose fits my personality very well.

I also love content marketing, as I like being useful, so by writing interesting articles, podcasting, making videos or sharing useful links on Twitter, I can attract attention without feeling like I'm 'marketing.' Many authors say "I could never do video or a podcast as I'm shy," but the truth is that when you make videos or audios, you're alone or with one other person, so it works well for introverts. So don't discard any ideas just yet. Here are some questions to consider so you can work out what kind of marketing might fit your personality.

- **How do you like to connect with people?** Do you enjoy large groups, parties, events or do you prefer one–on–one connection? When do you have energy for interaction? How can you utilize these natural preferences for marketing? Will you push yourself outside your comfort zone to achieve something specific?

- Do you like to be helpful and provide information? Or are you entertaining? Do you make people laugh? Are you inspiring?

- **Do you like images or words in terms of conveying ideas?** For example, a love of photography might skew you toward Pinterest or Instagram, or doing video instead of writing articles.

- **What sites do you hang out on right now for fun?** Do you love YouTube or Facebook or listening to podcasts already?

- **What broader interests do you have outside the world of your book?** For example, do you love dogs? Are you a parent? Scuba diver? Do you do a lot of research for your books? These aspects of your character can act as hooks for your marketing, leading people tangentially to your book.

You also need to think about your long-term career as a writer. Is your marketing just about one book, or are you building for the long term? How can you make marketing a sustainable part of your life?

When it all gets too much

This book is like an eat-all-you-like buffet. If you try to eat everything at once, you are just going to get sick. The same applies when you're in eighteen different Facebook groups, reading tons of books and listening to podcasts and getting advice from so many people that you end up overwhelmed and frantic, wondering why the hell you're bothering.

I definitely get overwhelmed sometimes, because the To Do list is never finished. There is always more we could read, or do, or share. You will always be missing out on something, because you just can't do everything. You have to choose.

Some days, it's best to switch everything off, step away from the Internet, turn away from whatever is driving you crazy and just rest. Read a book. Sleep. Go back to the pleasure of writing before you thought about marketing. Remember why you're doing this. And later, when you're rested, you can return to your marketing with more energy and a fresh perspective.

* * *

These are some of the mindset shifts for you to consider. As you read through this book, weigh up how each marketing idea fits with how you see yourself now and in the future. But also, challenge the way you feel and don't be afraid to try new things.

1.2 Polarities of marketing

"Sales and marketing done right isn't just a
cookie-cutter process; it's an art."

Kristine Kathryn Rusch, *Discoverability:*
Help Readers Find You In Today's World of Publishing

Book marketing is not a monolithic thing, it doesn't happen at one single time, and your marketing activities will change over your career as a writer.

There is no magic bullet, only a number of different options that you can utilize along your author journey. Here are some of the opposite polarities on the marketing scale that, along with your definition of success, will help shape your marketing activities. You will move up and down on these scales with every book and as you change over time. There is no 'right' way, just a series of choices that can result in multiple combinations. This is just an overview and I'll go into the details in subsequent chapters.

Short term vs. long term

Many new authors with only one book will focus on short-term sales spikes because they can't yet imagine a future with more books. I was exactly the same! Short-term sales are fantastic for that initial launch push, but they often cost money and are not sustainable over time. After all, once you hit the top of the charts, there's only one way to go from there.

If you want a long-term career as an author, you also need to think about long-term marketing. You want to build a sustainable baseline income, money that comes in from your books consistently every month. This comes from having more books on the market but also from building your email list and other marketing activities covered in Part 4.

Focused vs. eclectic

Some authors focus entirely on one brand, one genre and one type of marketing. They go deep and become an expert, ignoring everything else in their strategic direction.

I wish I could be like that sometimes! But the opposite is someone like me who likes to write in multiple genres, who has a bit of a magpie brain and likes to try different things over time, who can't focus on just one way of marketing.

Both can be successful, and because it often does come down to personality, it's important to avoid comparisonitis with other authors who do things differently. See my book *The Successful Author Mindset* if you are struggling with this or other mindset issues.

Income vs. brand building

Some marketing activities are about making direct income, whereas others are about brand building. For example, getting on a network TV show or a national radio show can be amazing for building awareness of your author name, and as social proof for your website. Having a physical book launch party at a swanky location might make the local paper, or give you some great photos for social media.

But if you want to make direct income, you'd be better off publishing a multi-book-boxset and using some paid ads to direct sales there.

Paid vs. free

I've spent nearly ten years building up an author platform using my time, not my money. It costs little to set up a professional website with an off-the-shelf theme, and it's free to write articles, or podcast, make videos and share on social media. It's free to self-publish on all the major platforms, and you can find out everything you need to know from free and cheap books and resources. You can definitely build an author platform and generate good sales from free marketing – but you will pay with your time.

If you are short on time and want to pay for marketing, you can spend whatever you like, from $5 a day on Facebook or Amazon Ads to hundreds of thousands for a TV advertising campaign or even just by ramping up those ads. Traditional publishers have been using paid advertising for years. They know that there is competition for attention, and to get ahead of the pack, you often have to have a coordinated marketing campaign. Many authors are now using paid marketing activities, as outlined in Part 3, alongside their longer-term platform-building. It's certainly how I use it.

The book vs. you

There are two main ways that your book can be discovered – through the book itself, or through you as the author.

Discovery through the book doesn't require you to have a Facebook page or an email list. These sales are driven by your book's metadata and the algorithms of the distributor, as well as paid advertising. They are based on keywords, book title, book cover, description, people's browsing history, the sales of your book, reviews and rankings in particular categories and everything else that exists within the online bookstore ecosystem.

Discovery through you as the author includes activities such as interviews, guest posting, social media activities, audio or video, speaking at events, networking, PR or staying in touch with readers through your email list.

You may have a different focus per book. For example, I recently launched a new sweet romance series that I co-wrote with my mum. It's under a pen-name that I'm not disclosing because I want to keep the audience segmented away from my thriller and non-fiction niches. We won't be doing any platform-building or blogging or podcasting or anything that involves us as authors. My mum is 70 and is not Internet savvy, so she doesn't want to do all that, and I'm already running two other active brands under my own name. So we are relying entirely on the books themselves plus paid advertising. This is quite common for authors using multiple pseudonyms, as it is hard to maintain multiple platforms, and it is definitely possible to make a decent living from books using only this method.

Compare this approach to how I run Joanna Penn, my non-fiction name, and J.F.Penn for thrillers. For both of these brands, my photo is everywhere, I blog and podcast and use multiple social media sites. I have a very active platform for both names. I use paid ads to supplement these activities, but my marketing is often centered more around me as the author.

Your very first book with no audience vs. later books when you have a readership

When you're first starting out, you have fewer options for book marketing. You need a significant number of reviews for promotion on the bigger paid email blast sites, like BookBub, so they might not be an option. You can use other types of paid ads, but if you only have one book and no sell-through to others under your author name, you will likely be out of pocket.

However, once you have a number of books, preferably in a series or aimed at the same target market, you will likely have an email list that you can use for marketing a new book, as well as readers ready to leave reviews. You will have a budget for paid ads, and you will be more confident of sell-through. You'll also be clearer on your author brand and your target market. This is the benefit of time and a longer-term focus, consistently growing your readership book on book, year on year. Trust me, it gets easier!

Traditional vs. indie publishing

This is all about control. If you are traditionally published, you will not be able to change the price on your book, or switch out the cover, or change the category, which are tactics that many indies do to rejuvenate sales. Some agile publishers will do this on your behalf, but most traditionally published authors focus on marketing through literary festivals, live events, relationships with book bloggers and PR. Indie authors often focus online, with paid advertising, price promotions, boxsets and other activities that require control of the book.

Stand-alone vs. series

A few years ago, I co-wrote *Risen Gods* with J. Thorn. It's a stand-alone dark fantasy thriller set in New Zealand at the beginning of an apocalyptic event. It gets amazing reviews, but it's tough to sell. Compare that to my main ARKANE series, which has nine novels right now, with more to come. It's much easier to market as I have a free first in series book on all platforms, which gets people into the series every day. If people enjoy the first book, they are more likely to read the next one. I also have boxsets and can afford to do price promotion on earlier books to lead people into the series. The principle is the same with non-fiction.

If you write stand-alones, consider what might tie them together, for example, sense of place, or the same target market, like my Books for Writers, which can be read separately, but work together as a non-fiction series.

Exclusive vs. wide

Your marketing will differ depending on where and how you publish. If you are exclusive to Amazon with the KDP Select program, then you will have visibility in the Kindle Unlimited (KU) ecosystem, which has become its own market. KU readers pay a set amount per month and can read as many books as they like – as long as those books are in KU. Some of them may buy other books, but their preference will be to borrow, rather than buy. These are high-volume readers who can devour a series quickly, giving you a lot of page reads and a good author income. There are also specific KU marketing options like free days and Countdown deals, plus some authors claim evidence of an algorithm preference for books in KU.

However, if you're exclusive to Amazon, you miss out of the huge audience that shops on Kobo, Apple Books, Barnes & Noble Nook and all the other retailers that are springing up in markets around the world, as well as the merchandising opportunities there.

Publish fast vs. publish slowly

Publishing fast is a form of marketing in itself, because the Amazon algorithms favor new content, much as Google does. Some authors choose to write and publish at a faster pace, within a 30, 60 or 90 day period, using email lists and paid promotions to keep their books high in the rankings. We'll cover this more in chapter 3.7.

Most authors choose to write and publish over a longer time-frame, with an annual or bi-annual schedule, using sporadic launch promotions and longer-term marketing tactics.

Writing to market vs. writing the book of your heart

> "Writing to market is picking an under-served genre that you know has a voracious appetite, and then giving that market exactly what it wants."
>
> Chris Fox, *Write to Market*

Writing to market is baking the marketing into the book by writing something that will sell because there is an audience waiting to devour it. This suits writers who can write fast and adapt to new niches, but also where the author reads and loves something about the genre. A great example is LitRPG, which features characters trapped within MMOs (massively multiplayer online role-playing games). A lot of indie science fiction and fantasy authors, who are also gamers, got into this niche quickly, writing books to this market and some of them did incredibly well.

This tactic works until the sub-category on Amazon becomes saturated, then the market becomes harder to sell in, and some writers move onto other genres.

"Be an artist: write what you love. When you're done, *then* worry about marketing it."

Kristine Kathryn Rusch, *Discoverability*

Most authors start out writing the book of their heart, the book their muse wants them to write, the book that has been itching for years to be created. They write that book without any thought of marketing and worry about reaching readers later. Many will continue in this vein, satisfying artistic needs before marketing considerations.

This polarity can also be described as **writing for readers vs. writing for yourself**. The purest example is poetry, because you write it for the love of language, to nurture your creative soul, rather than for money. Poetry is hard to market and is not a top-selling niche, so you will always write it for you. If you want to write for readers, then check Amazon or AuthorEarnings.com for the top-selling genres and you will find plenty of voracious readers for your words.

It's important to understand that you can do both over your author career, and your approach will differ per book over time. Many authors start out writing because they have a burning idea they want to get into the world and they are passionate about a particular niche. Later, they may write to market, especially if they are now writing for a living. You gotta pay those bills!

I do both. My fiction as J.F.Penn is all written for the Muse, each project born from my curiosity. Much of my nonfiction, including this book, is written to help others on the author journey. I have an audience who want this book, so in a sense, it is written to market.

Neither option is 'better' than the other. What's so fantastic about the creative world we live in now is that there's room for writers of all types, and many more authors are making a living with their words.

Online vs. offline. Global vs. local

Offline marketing is anything you do in person, for example, speaking at a local event about your book. It might be running a class at a school to promote your children's book, or attending a networking event, or speaking at a literary festival or a book club at a library. The benefits of this type of marketing include immediate sales and local brand building, as well as the possibility to develop a community and other author friends.

The problem with offline marketing is that it is not scalable. You can only reach the people who are physically with you at that moment. Compare that to spending the same amount of time writing a blog post that could touch thousands online in multiple countries, or going on a podcast interview that could reach a global market, or curating photos on your Instagram channel within your niche. I choose to spend most of my marketing time and budget online in order to grow a global audience, but I also do a few speaking events and writers' festivals every year. I do both, but I focus on global, online marketing as the most effective and scalable use of my time.

Introvert vs. extrovert

Thanks to *Quiet* by Susan Cain, many writers are happily claiming their introversion. I'm an introvert, which means I get my energy from being alone. I hate small talk and large groups. I'd rather think than speak, and write rather than talk. I rarely answer the phone. I'm INFJ on the Myers

Briggs scale, and many authors fit a similar model. This also means that conferences and events are tiring, so I can't do too many of them a year. If you're like me, then we're super lucky these days, because online marketing suits introverts. We can attract an audience online and connect with readers, while still spending time alone.

In contrast, extroverts get their energy from people, so live events are fun and energizing for them and may be a much better way to market and connect than it is for introverts.

Ebook vs. print

I recommend you have both available, but different forms of marketing suit the different formats. This relates to online and offline above because print books often sell very well at live events and speakers can do well with 'back-of-the-room' sales. Non-fiction also sells better in print and I certainly find that December sales of print are always better because of the gift season.

Ebook-specific marketing includes free promotions, which can't be done with print books because there is always a cost of production and shipping. So you can give away thousands of free books, and it won't cost you anything, whereas most authors put a cap on the number of print books they give away.

Fiction vs. non-fiction

My non-fiction marketing as Joanna Penn is different to how I market my fiction as J.F.Penn. For non-fiction, I have a blog and a podcast. I curate information on social media and I do live speaking events. For J.F.Penn, I concentrate on writing a series in a popular genre, using a perma-free first in series, utilizing paid ads and price promotions, boxsets and networking with other authors in the genre. For both, I concentrate on building an email list of readers, but they are quite different in the focus of marketing activities.

Your own name vs. a pseudonym

If you are writing books under a version of your name, as I do for Joanna Penn and J.F.Penn, then you can use your own face, your photos and details about your life in your marketing. You can do videos and audio and PR and generally be more open. Platform-building is easy and sustainable over time.

If you're writing books under a pseudonym that you want to keep secret or separate from your name, as I do for the sweet romance, then platform-building is difficult. If you don't want to use your face or your photos or your voice, then you're more likely to focus on writing a series, price promotions and paid ads.

Data focused vs. people focused

Marketing is diverging into two poles: the kind that uses data analytics to drive decision-making and advertising, and the kind that focuses on attracting like-minded people.

Data focused marketing includes tools that dig down into the Amazon sub-categories, looking for under-served niches and focusing on algorithm changes, as well as spreadsheets for keyword focus, return-on-investment (ROI) and tweaking website SEO to reach more readers.

People focused marketing includes speaking, collaboration, writing articles, podcasting, making videos or using images to attract like-minded people and then developing a relationship with them over time.

There is room for both, but they suit different people, and you may find one more attractive than the other.

Push marketing vs. pull marketing

Push marketing is also known as interruption marketing, things like paid advertising that push your work in front of people. Pull marketing is about attraction and permission, drawing people to you by providing useful, entertaining or inspiring content and developing a relationship that makes them want to buy from you over time.

* * *

These are some of the polarities that you will navigate through your book marketing journey over time. Think of them all as sliding scales that you move up and down along the way, focusing on different aspects over time. Remember, there is no magic bullet when it comes to marketing, only what is the right thing for you and your book over time.

1.3 When to start marketing and how to balance your time

There are different opinions on when to start marketing, and there are no correct answers. These are my thoughts based on my experience and observing other authors at all stages of the author journey.

If you have a book or more out already, then what are you waiting for? Everything in this book is fair game.

If you are writing your first novel

I speak at a lot of author events, and get asked a lot of questions. So many writers get hung up on the minutiae of marketing when they don't even have a book yet. They might be asking about the intricacies of Amazon Ads before they've even finished chapter three. But most people who start writing a book never finish it, so you need to spend all your time and energy getting it done so you are not one of them.

I also found that it took me several novels before I found my voice and was able to let go of the self-censorship that was holding me back. I ended up changing my author name for my third novel because I could see my audience was so different.

My recommendation if you are only writing fiction is to wait until your manuscript is with an editor before you consider marketing options. In that way, you will know that you are going to make it to publication and you should have more of an idea what genre you're writing in.

If you want to get going now, then start by building relationships online with other authors in your genre through
social networks. These relationships often grow into something more substantial over time, and you can learn from
what others are doing. But don't distract yourself from
writing. Finishing the book is always the most important
thing. You have nothing to market if you don't have a book!

If you are writing your first non-fiction book

It's much easier to build a non-fiction platform before the
book is launched because it's usually based on a topic or
specific niche. In fact, many non-fiction authors start out
with a business or speaking or another form of income first
before they decide to write a book.

You could start blogging about your topic or start a podcast
around your niche as a way to build an audience before the
book is out. It's certainly not a prerequisite by any means,
but it can help loosen up your writing style and make it
easier to connect with influencers in the market.

How to balance your time

"How we spend our days is, of course,
how we spend our lives."

Annie Dillard

One of the most common questions I get asked is, "How
do you balance your time between writing and marketing,
as well as the rest of life?" But marketing doesn't have to

cannibalize your writing, because there are two kinds of time.

Creative time

This is when you have the energy to be at your creative best and when I suggest you write and produce. This is not marketing or email or social media time. It's for writing the first or the next book.

It may take you some effort to work out, but for me, it's always the morning. When I had a full-time job, I would get up at 5 a.m. to write before work, because after work, I had nothing left. I was exhausted. These days, it's still the morning, and in fact, as I write this, I'm at my usual café with my noise-cancelling headphones on doing my creative morning slot.

But everyone has different approaches, so pick whatever time is right for you.

This doesn't mean that you can magically stream gorgeous-ness onto the page at that time every day, because creativity is hard work, with occasional moments of flow. But mostly, it's about getting your butt in that chair and writing words that you can later edit into something fantastic.

So decide on your creative time and then make sure that you use that time to create something new in the world. Put that slot into your schedule or your calendar. Make an appointment with yourself as you would with a business colleague or a friend for lunch or your yoga class or your kids' events. Is your writing time not as important as those other things? If it isn't, then you should probably reassess wanting to be a writer.

Downtime

Then there is the other time that is not taken up by your family, or work commitments when you're mentally tired and not feeling creative. This is where you can manage your marketing and the learning required to develop marketing skills.

When I worked full time, this was any time after work, or during any breaks I managed to snatch during the day. Count the number of hours a week you watch TV because you're exhausted and then take half of those for your book marketing time. For me, this is in the afternoon or evening, when I have finished my creative work.

What will you give up in order to make time?

We all have the same number of hours in the day, so you have to decide what you will do with yours. When I decided to become a full-time author, I was so miserable at my day job that I was willing to do anything to change my life.

We got rid of the TV, and I actively chose to consume less media and focus on creation rather than consumption. We still watch specific shows but actively choose what we watch and limit the number of hours. How many hours a day are you passively consuming content? You might be able to free up several hours per night, or even just one extra hour that you can use productively. If you're a night owl, then use this time to write and your early morning slot for a marketing session.

I also gave up 20% of my income in exchange for time. I moved to four days a week at work, so that I could spend an extra day on writing and marketing. I also worked pretty much every weekend on my author business, cutting out a lot of social commitments and other hobbies. This was a serious career change for me, and I was willing to invest in it.

You have to decide on your goals and take control of your life and your time. That's it. It's simple, but like so many things, it's not easy. **How much do you want this?**

The truth is that no one ever has enough time to do everything. The To Do list is never empty. The work of an author is never over. It is not a 9-5 experience where you can drop it all when you get home. It's a constant stream of ideas that you want to write about, a myriad of marketing possibilities … and then there's real life to fit in! So keep coming back to why you are doing this. What is your definition of success and what will you give up to achieve that?

PART 2:
Your Book
Fundamentals

2.1 Prerequisites for success

If you don't get these prerequisites right, marketing can be a waste of time. So don't skip this section!

(1) Produce a quality finished product

What defines a "good" book is up to the reader. 125 million readers loved *50 Shades of Grey*, whereas the latest literary prize-winner barely sells a fraction of that, yet is lauded by the media. So this is no comment on what genre you choose to write, but whatever it is, you should aim to create a quality finished product that your readers will enjoy.

Your book is competing with millions of others out there, and it needs to stand alongside the bestsellers in your genre. You also want to produce the best book you can for your sense of pride, and respect your readers enough to care about their experience. This means spending time on your writing craft and using professional editors and proofreaders to ensure your book is the best it can be, plus using professional cover design to attract your target readers.

Mega-bestselling indie author Hugh Howey explains why you need editing processes in order to self-publish quality material.

> "**The biggest barrier to releasing quality material is probably impatience.** You have a work that feels pretty good; you're exhausted; you want to move on; you might be a bit delusional about how good it really is; so you hit publish. Nobody steps in and tells you to make it better, to do another pass, to get a better cover, to write a better blurb, to hire

or trade for some editing, to beg or trade for some beta reading. You simply jump the gun."

So curb your impatience and hire some professionals. You can find my list of editors and proofreaders at:

www.TheCreativePenn.com/editors

(2) Understand your target market

Most new writers think that their book will appeal to everyone in the world, but the truth is that most people aren't interested or won't like your book. The trick is to find those who *will* be interested. There are a number of ways to do this:

(a) Find your comparison authors

If you have an agent, you will need to discuss 'comps' or comparison authors, and if you self-publish, you need to know this too. The best way to hook into an existing niche in a reader's mind is to relate your book to existing products out there. So I say that people who like James Rollins or Dan Brown will enjoy my *ARKANE* books because they are fast-paced thrillers with religious and historical themes as well as international locations. Yes, that will also turn some readers off, but that's fine because your book is not for everyone!

You can also pick two authors or ideas and meld them together. I love Scott Sigler's description of his galactic football league books as *The Godfather meets Any Given Sunday*. My ARKANE books are *Dan Brown meets Lara Croft*. The reader knows what they're getting.

It's best to try and identify 5-10 books or authors similar to yours, or more if you can. Start to keep a list and if possible, copy and paste the covers and sales descriptions into a reference document, because they will be useful as models for your marketing later.

(b) Understand where your potential customers hang out

Once you know your target market, then you can look at where they usually browse or look for content. If you are writing a book on organic tomatoes, it might be organic gardening or healthy eating blogs and magazines, or sites/publications that review other similar books.

For fiction, it might be email lists that target those readers e.g. BookBub or sites/publications that review other similar books e.g. genre book bloggers

I'll go into this in a lot more detail later on, but at this point, you want to focus on understanding who your audience are and where they hang out.

(c) Figure out which category or genre your book fits into on the retail stores

This is much easier for non-fiction. For example, you are an organic tomato enthusiast and you want to write a book on the subject. Who is the target audience for this book? Obviously, this will be organic tomato enthusiasts, but also organic gardeners in general, or foodie/gourmet types. They hang out in gardening or hobby categories.

For fiction, this is all about genre. Your specific target market will be in Thriller or Romance or Sci-Fi or within Literary Fiction or a mash-up between audiences. You can drill down into these using the Categories on Amazon. Some categories have more voracious readers than others.

If you need help deciding on sub-categories to target on Amazon, check out the reports on K-lytics:

www.TheCreativePenn.com/genre

You can also find a free tutorial on choosing sub-categories at: TheCreativePenn.com/rocketcategories

There are expectations and 'rules' within each of these categories that you need to fulfill in order to satisfy the demands of those particular readers, and knowing where your book will sit on the virtual shelf is critical.

(3) Make sure your book cover design is genre-specific

Your book cover is one of the most important marketing assets you have. It catches a reader's eye as they browse, and people *do* judge a book by its cover, at least determining whether to read the sales description or check out a sample. You also use your cover as part of your advertising and author platform, so it has to reflect the promise to the reader. Trust me on this, you will use that book cover in so many places, it is well worth the investment in a professional design.

The exercise in identifying your comparison authors will help with this. You can identify similar elements of bestselling books and provide those examples to your cover designer as a starting point. There are very clear design elements for genre books, e.g. if it has a dragon on it, the book is likely to be fantasy. Readers take cues from these images, and it is critical to give the right impression.

One of the best things about being self-published is control of the publishing process, so if your cover isn't right, or you just want to change it up, you can easily swap it out for a new one. I've changed covers on many of my books, and even the titles on some of them, and it's something traditional publishing often does to refresh the sales of older books.

You can find a list of recommended book cover designers as well as do-it-yourself options at:

www.TheCreativePenn.com/bookcoverdesign

2.2 Book sales description

It's a mammoth task to write a whole book, but it's also a challenge to turn it into a sales description that makes readers want to buy now and start reading immediately.

Copywriting is writing text with the purpose of marketing or selling, and it is quite different to the writing skills that authors usually rely on. If you're traditionally published, your publisher will do the sales description for you, but you won't be able to change it. If you're indie, you have to do it yourself (or pay someone to do it for you), but luckily, you can also change it whenever you like. Most indies will change their sales description multiple times, so just get started, and you can finesse it later.

Start by revisiting your comparison titles and copy out the book sales description for each. This will give you a sense of the language used and how the description is structured. It's not a summary of the book, it's an advert that will hopefully make the reader want to buy.

Fiction sales descriptions

Most novels have a hook in the headline, something that makes the reader intrigued and want to know more. This hook needs to be genre-specific and preferably emotional in some way. For example, my first line for *Stone of Fire* is:

> A power kept secret for 2000 years. A woman who stands to lose everything.

It's a high-stakes religious conspiracy thriller in the tradition of Dan Brown, and you should get that sense straightaway.

Fiction sales descriptions usually name and describe the main characters as well as the inciting incident, the thing that sets the plot in motion and the start of the emotional journey. They might also open up the aspects of the antagonist or the conflict that will get in the way of what the character wants, for example, the deadly storm, the abusive ex, or the shadowy government forces.

They also use hyperbole, words that seem over-the-top or clichéd, but they are used for a reason. That's why so many crime novels are chilling or deadly, and so many thrillers are action-packed with a race against time. Traditional publishers have been doing this for many years, so model the books that are selling in your genre, although, of course, don't plagiarize and make sure the language you use is right for your book.

The sales description often ends with a question that makes the reader want to answer it by reading the book. Don't give too much of the plot away, but intrigue people enough that they want to read on.

BookBub did a study on sales descriptions by split testing variants and discovered that mentioning awards an author had won increased click-through. They also recommend using sub-category genres in the text e.g. psychological thriller instead of just thriller, as well as using ellipses at the end of a sentence, and avoiding too many character names.

You can find the study at:

www.TheCreativePenn.com/bookbubAB

Non-fiction sales descriptions

What is the problem that your book will solve for the reader? What question are you answering?

The goal of a non-fiction book is usually to solve a particular problem for a reader. The customer is searching for answers to their problem, and they need to know that your book addresses that specifically. It has to be worth them buying the book. You can use that right at the top of the sales description in the form of a question. For this book, I used "Do you want to sell more books and reach more readers?"

Your answer is presumably 'yes,' which is why you're reading this book. It's all about empathy with your reader. What problem do *they* have? What language will *they* resonate with?

For example, I talked to a clinical psychologist with a book on cognitive behavioral therapy (CBT) that wasn't selling. His sales description was overly technical about the therapy itself, whereas actually, readers would be searching for help with their problem, so his hook should be "Do you need help with depression or anxiety?" rather than "Do you need CBT?"

Once you have identified the problem, you can write about why you're the person to help and what the book includes. You need to establish your expertise. The reader needs to know that not only does this book solve the problem, but that they can trust you to help.

You can include a table of contents, but it might be best to condense the various parts with mini-headlines that entice the reader even more. You can also use bullet-point formatting, which makes it easier to read. The phrasing here is important, for example, use "In this book, you will discover," rather than "In this book, I will teach." The word 'you' is incredibly important in copywriting and keeps the focus on the reader, because they are thinking, "What's in it for me?"

Blurbs from other authors and media

One study by BookBub found that a quote from a well-known author boosted click-through rate by 22%. A quote from an author like Stephen King will get a better click-through than a quote from a publication like Publishers Weekly. So quotes from well-known authors are great if you can get them and you should put them right after your headline. But let's face it, most of us won't get a cover quote from the biggest names in our genre.

If you have quotes from less well-known authors or blogs, put them in the editorial review section which you can access through Amazon Author Central, covered in chapter 2.5.

Formatting and testing

You can format your sales description with basic HTML, which will give you larger headlines, sub-heads and bullets.

I use a formatting tool from Kindlepreneur which enables me to display the headline at a different font size and use italics, spacing and bullet points.

You can find it at: TheCreativePenn.com/rocketdescription

You can test different changes to your sales description over time, and even if you don't want to do that, make a note in your calendar to review your sales descriptions every six months, or at least annually, because things change, you change, and you will likely update it over time.

* * *

If you want to know more about writing your book sales description, I recommend *How to Write a Sizzling Synopsis* by Bryan Cohen. You can also listen to an interview with him at www.TheCreativePenn.com/bryancohen

2.3 Choose the right categories and keywords

You might not want to put your book in a box or a genre or a category, but you have to, because that's how a lot of readers find their next book. Many authors resist this categorization, and it is difficult when you first start out, but it's a fundamental of book marketing, so you need to understand and use it for your book. I know words like metadata, keywords, search engine optimization and algorithms can blow people's minds, but this side of things is an important part of being an indie author!

Choose the right category

The category or genre reader has expectations, and if you don't meet them, they will be disappointed, and you'll get bad reviews. That's not to say that you need to follow any specific rules while you're writing, but when you publish the book, you will have to choose which categories to use, and they need to be meaningful. If you have a publisher, they will do this for you, but it's best to discuss it with them anyway.

It's important to match reader expectations and the promise of what your book delivers with what your book is actually about. There is no point having a book with a swirly, girly pink chic-lit cover in the horror category. It won't sell, however good it is.

If you can, choose a category that fits your book *and* is easier to rank in. You get between two and ten categories, depending on the platform you're publishing to. On Amazon, you can also get into extra categories through using your keywords to target Browse Categories. You can find a list at www.TheCreativePenn.com/browse. You can also email the help team through Amazon Author Central and ask for your book to be moved to categories if they are not selectable.

If you're struggling with deciding on your categories, go back to your list of comparison authors and books.

Check what categories they are in and then spend some time looking at whether your book fits there or what the other options could be.

This can be time-consuming to do manually and person-ally, I'd rather spend my time researching obscure artifacts in dusty museums, writing more books, or just getting on with life. Perhaps you feel that way too! I suspect this is all too common in the indie author community right now, because we want to use data, but we aren't too keen on the process for getting it or working out how to use it.

So if you'd rather use a tool to help you, check out **K-lytics,** which has some fantastic reasonably priced genre reports that go into the best target sub-categories to use as well as recommendations for comparison authors, keywords and more. Alex, who runs K-lytics, is an absolute data geek and he spends his time combing the Amazon US rankings and categories for insights that will help. He loves this stuff – so you don't have to!

If you need help deciding on sub-categories to target on Amazon, check out the reports on K-lytics:

www.TheCreativePenn.com/genre

You can also find a free tutorial on choosing sub-categories at TheCreativePenn.com/rocketcategories

Choosing the right keywords

Keywords and search engine optimization have been considered important for a long time in the online world, particularly for ranking on the first few pages of the search engines so that people can find you.

But these principles are also important for your book page on the retail stores. They make up a critical part of the metadata that is crucial in the discoverability of your book. I also realize this might sound like gobbledegook, so I will explain further using the example of my non-fiction book, and also my novels, because keywords are just as important for fiction authors.

What is a keyword?

A keyword is a word or phrase that is associated with your book. It's based on the words that people use to search online, and this is a crucial aspect, because often the language *you* use is not the language that your customers might use. For example, many of us use the terms 'indie author' or 'indie publishing,' but a new author who is not yet in the tribe would only recognize 'publishing' or 'self-publishing.'

Importantly, a keyword is not just one word, and that is critical to remember as you go through the following process. For example, my thriller novel *Ark of Blood* is associated with the keyword "ark of the covenant" and my non-fiction book with "career change."

So, how do you come up with keywords for your book and how do you use them?

(1) Check the Browse Category lists for keywords that will get you into categories

For example, 'conspiracy thriller' can be used in the keyword section to get into that sub-category on the Amazon store, even though you can't select it in the KDP area for categories. You can find a list of these at:

www.TheCreativePenn.com/browse

(2) Generate words and phrases to use as keywords

Amazon is a search engine for people who want to buy things, including your book! It has an auto-populate tool that enables you to see a drop-down of specific words or phrases. Just start typing something into the search bar, and you'll get a drop-down. Make sure that you're in the Books/Kindle store if you want to narrow the search down.

Try it now. Go to Amazon and start typing a word or phrase you want to check into the search bar. For example, I typed in 'career c' and it came up with all kinds of phrases that started that way: career coaching books, career catapult, career code, career change, career counseling, and others.

This can help you with more than just keywords for your existing book. It can also help you come up with ideas for new topics, particularly with non-fiction.

Make a list of all the words and phrases that are associated with your book. For fiction, that might include themes, places, things and anything concrete that you can hang your book off.

For *Ark of Blood*, that might include ark of the covenant, Israel, Jerusalem, freemasons – as those are some themes and places in the book, so people searching for those things might be interested in it. For my non-fiction book, *Career Change*, I used career change, what should I do with my life, career help, hate my job, career match, career books, choosing a career.

Try to be as specific as possible in order to find your correct target audience. For example, the word 'pain' could relate to back pain, pain of grief, pain of divorce, and many more options, so use keyword phrases where possible.

You can also use various tools to help you generate possible keyword options (which you can also use for marketing as covered in chapter 3.5).

KDP Rocket will help you analyze categories and keyword ideas in real time and has specific options for Amazon Ads. Check it out at www.TheCreativePenn.com/rocket

Google has a Keyword Search Tool that you can use to discover what search terms people are using and what are the most popular at adwords.google.com/KeywordPlanner. It is primarily used for people working on advertising terms, so you do need to create an ad account, although you don't need to spend any money to use the tool. You can also use tools like KeywordTool.io, and other options appear all the time.

(3) Add the keywords into your book metadata

Once you have a list of keywords, you can use these in your book metadata, the fields that the publishing sites use to categorize your book.

You can also use keywords in your book title, sub-title and in your book description and editorial reviews area. It's important to note that your cover must include the title that you use, so you can't just stuff it full of keywords. Your text should be human-focused first.

Non-fiction authors can use this type of research to make a decision on their book title or, at least, their sub-title. There's no point in your title meaning something to you but nothing to anyone else. Too often, authors will decide on a title that has emotional resonance for them, but they would be better off using specific keywords that will help customers find them more easily.

How a keyword change in my book title boosted sales 10x

I wrote my first non-fiction book as a labor of love and the book of my heart. I spent 13 years as a miserable business consultant, a cubicle slave like so many others. In 2006, I embarked on a journey to find work I could be passionate about because I felt like I was wasting my life. In 2008, I published the result of that journey in *How to Enjoy your Job ... or Get a New One.*

Yes, seriously. That was my brilliant book title! But it turns out that most people don't want to enjoy their job.

As I started to learn about book marketing, I discovered the importance of keywords. I did some keyword searches on Amazon and also checked the number of monthly searches on Google. 'How to enjoy your job' had 5,400 global monthly searches, whereas 'career change' had 165,000 global monthly searches. I decided to change my title as well as the cover, and in 2012, after learning a lot more about craft as well as book marketing, I rewrote and republished the book as *Career Change: Stop Hating your Job, Discover What you Really Want to do with your Life and Start Doing it!*

Sales increased by a factor of ten, which is significant even though the overall sales are pretty small for most of the year, spiking in January during self-help season. I don't speak on this topic, and it doesn't fit with my other non-fiction books, so the sales are mainly due to people searching for that keyword.

I also continue to get media attention based on journalists searching for 'career change' and finding the book online. I've featured as a career change expert on national TV and radio in Australia and the UK, as well as in national newspapers and local papers. It's also interesting to note that none of them asked who I was published by, so being self-published is no barrier to media attention as long as your product (and you) are professional. Of course, it's important to note that there was no sales spike from the extra media attention, but it's good for social proof.

Categories and keywords are critical for visibility in the online bookstores, so it's well worth putting in some effort here to work out where your book fits.

2.4 Amazon Author Central

Whether you are traditionally published or self-published, you should be setting up your Author Central account as soon as your book is available on Amazon, because you can play around with your sales page formatting and add other metadata as well as add images and videos to your Author Page and book details. If you have books in translation, you can also get your bio translated and add that to the specific country Author Central site.

Why use Amazon Author Central?

You can set up an **author page** including your photo, blog posts, videos, Twitter feed and other materials that promote your work as well as a bio that tells people about you. It's the page that appears for your Author Name on Amazon when people click on your name.

You can **split one Author Central account into multiple pen-names** to ensure that your books appear on different author pages. I have J.F.Penn for fiction and Joanna Penn for non-fiction with different author data for each.

You can **re-format your book sales description** so that it is nicely spaced out, as well as adding bold, underlining and other formatting. For changes to your ebook sales description, it's best to use the KDP platform rather than Author Central.

You can **add more metadata for your books** like Author Bio, From the Author, and reviews, which can add more keyword-rich information and social proof to your book.

You can view **book sales tracking graphs** so that you can see your books' performance over time. You can also get

great help from the Contact Us page, which I have found useful for linking versions of books e.g. Kindle and print, and any other issues.

How to use Amazon Author Central

You can set up this page through Author Central at:

author.amazon.com

Sign in using the same Amazon email address that you use for publishing. Then start by adding books to your bibliography, verifying that they are your titles and populating your bio.

They may take a few days to appear, since Amazon validates that you have the right to the book. You can start populating your author page right away, and once that is done, it will appear in the Amazon search for your author name within a few days.

Hopefully, the other online book retail sites will follow suit with similar author pages in the future, as this offers authors more control over grouping books and a way for readers to find more books by an author they like.

2.5 Sampling. Why your first few pages are so important

A reader has made it to your book page, and they like the look of the cover and the description. What do they do next?

In a physical store, they might check the first few pages. But online, ebook readers will download a sample, or they will check a few pages in preview or Look Inside. So it is critical that you get your first chapters honed to perfection and hook the reader early.

How ebook readers shop and the importance of sampling

An author at a conference recently asked me for tips on publishing ebooks and then said that he didn't read on a digital device. I was gobsmacked, because how else are you going to know if there are problems until you start getting one-star reviews?

When you publish a print book, don't you buy it immediately to test the process and the quality? So why not do the same for your ebook? If you're going to publish ebooks, I believe that you should at least try the digital shopping and reading experience. You can even free apps for PC, Mac, tablet or mobile devices if you don't want to buy a dedicated ebook reading device. It's also important to understand how ebook readers shop, because they are high-volume consumers and likely make up the bulk of your digital sales.

How do ebook readers shop for books?

I'll use myself as an example, as I read digitally 95% of the time on a Kindle Paperwhite and through the Kindle app on my iPhone. I am also a voracious reader, getting through three books per week, more on holidays. I'm also a member of Amazon Prime and Kindle Unlimited.

I hear about a book through a podcast, or I see one in a physical bookstore, or see a review or a recommendation on social media, or find something I like in the Amazon store Top rankings for categories I prefer. I often surf for fun in the Last 30 Days area. I also subscribe to BookBub.com for ebook promotions, and I buy from that occasionally.

If the book is available as an ebook, I download the sample right away. If it's in KU, I might borrow immediately. If the book isn't available as an ebook, 99% of the time I won't buy it unless it's an author I'm committed to. If I really want it, I'll add it to my WishList, which I check periodically to see if ebook versions have become available.

In between books I'm currently reading, I go through my samples. If I make it to the end of the sample, I will usually buy the book, because I'm hooked. If I don't, I delete the sample. I usually give a book three clicks of my Kindle before I delete it or return it if it's in KU. Harsh, maybe, but life is too short to read books that don't call to you, and many readers are the same as me.

Remember: the reader doesn't care about you. They just want a satisfying read.

So your marketing efforts, your book cover, your book description and reviews have helped your book to get this far, but it is the sample that leads a reader like me to buy. I probably delete 75% of my samples, so I have a harsh approach, but I don't think I'm untypical for a high-volume ebook reader.

Make sure that your sample makes the reader want to buy

This is genre/category specific, but basically, the sample must offer a taste of the experience to come. Your book has to start with something that hooks the reader. This isn't new advice. Noah Lukeman's *The First 5 Pages* covered this years ago for the traditional publishing industry. If you want an agent, the first page has to hook them, and readers of print in bookstores may browse the first page. Because there are so many ebooks available, readers are increasingly unforgiving if a book doesn't fit what they are looking for. Here are some tips.

Get into the meat as soon as possible.

Put all the quotes, acknowledgments, foreword, and extra stuff at the back, not within the sample. I downloaded an anthology of Angela Carter short stories and was annoyed to find that the entire sample was an essay about her work written by someone else. The stories didn't come until later. I deleted that and bought a different edition.

During the editing process, make sure you pay particular attention to what will hook the reader. If the book is non-fiction, what is the problem you're solving? If it's fiction, why would the reader read on? How have you caught their attention? What loops have you opened mentally near the beginning of the book that they must close by reading on?

Make sure that the formatting is easy to read throughout.

I have deleted samples straight away when they included coding errors. It denotes a lack of respect for the reader. This is why you need to test your files. Curiously this has happened more often with traditionally published books than indie ones. One book I downloaded was entirely formatted in Bold. Did no one even check it before publishing? Italics are also harder to read in ebooks so don't go crazy with them.

2.6 The pros and cons of exclusivity

"Amazon is the largest bookstore in the world.
The second largest is Kindle Unlimited."

Nick Webb, USA Today bestselling science
fiction author, quoted from the Science Fiction
and Fantasy Marketing Podcast

Exclusivity for authors means choosing to publish only on Amazon, and when authors refer to publishing wide, it means their books are available on other stores.

What are KDP Select and Kindle Unlimited?

KDP Select is an opt-in program available to authors who publish through the Amazon KDP dashboard as well as traditionally published authors who negotiate through agents and publishers. There is a check-box per book, and you opt in for 90 days of exclusivity, which is automatically rolled into the next 90 days unless you specifically opt out. To be clear, this means you can't publish the book on any other platform, including your own website, or in any boxsets, during this period.

If you opt in to KDP Select, your books are available in Kindle Unlimited (KU), which is a subscription program. Readers pay a fixed amount per month and can borrow and read unlimited books. It's considered the Netflix for books and encourages unlimited reading within the platform, attracting hardcore readers who would usually have to pay a lot more to read that much. Indie authors can only be in KU if they opt in with KDP Select as above, although some exceptions are made for big sellers. Authors are paid per page read based on a fixed monthly pool of money that is announced every month.

What are KU readers like?

In April 2017, Written Word Media produced a report on Kindle Unlimited readers based on a survey. They found that KU subscribers are avid readers, with 71% reading more than five books per month. They are more likely to review books they've read than non-KU subscribers and 77% purchase books outside of KU if they like the author. 35% of KU readers cite romance as their favorite genre, but genres dominated by traditionally published big name authors like James Patterson in Mystery/Thriller are less likely to be in KU.

75% of surveyed KU readers read on a phone, or a tablet, which means that back matter linking to your email list signup can be easily accessed, and effective cover design is even more important. You can find the whole report at www.TheCreativePenn.com/KUreport

The benefits of exclusivity

KU is its own ecosystem at this point, with a **sub-set of readers who only buy within the program**. If you don't have any books in KU, then you are missing out on this group of readers. Estimates based on the monthly payout put the numbers of KU readers at around three million, although Amazon doesn't share exact figures. The program is being rolled out in the biggest book markets globally, so the number of readers is increasing.

Discoverability is easier because anecdotal evidence suggests that the algorithms favor books in KU. There are also promotional options every 90 days including five days of free promotion, which can be good for getting reviews, and **Kindle Countdown Deals**, time-bound promotional discounting for your book.

For **some international markets**, you can only get 70% royalty if your book is in KU. As of 2017, this is applicable for Japan, India, Brazil and Mexico. If you're not in KU, you can only get 35% in these markets, even though you might get 70% in the other countries. Although these are not significant markets for most indie authors right now, they are a big focus for global growth.

Easier to manage changes.

Timing promotional price changes across stores is one of the big pain points if you publish wide. You can schedule a price change on Kobo and Apple Books, but Nook can take a few days, and Amazon's speed of change varies between 4-72 hours. Similarly, if you want to change back matter or fix a typo, you have to do it multiple times on multiple stores. Of course, you can use services like Smashwords or Draft2Digital and update once for all platforms, but I prefer to publish directly for the extra metadata fields I get on the various platforms. If you are exclusive to Amazon, you only have to manage one site and one set of changes per book.

The drawbacks to exclusivity

Missing out on the global growth of digital markets.

Amazon may be the biggest player in the US and UK, but there are other retail stores and devices that dominate in other countries. Germany has the Tolino, an ebook reader and associated stores that are run by a group of German publishers and they have a significant chunk of the market. My sales in Canada primarily come from Kobo, and both Kobo and Apple Books break sales down into 50+ countries. We haven't even got started in the massive Asian markets yet!

The Compound Effect.

By going direct to Apple Books and Kobo, I have started to grow an audience there, and my income ticks up as their ecosystems discover my books. *The Compound Effect* by Darren Hardy is a fantastic book that describes how little actions taken every day can add up over time to massive change, or massive impact over years. You can't expect to load your books up on Kobo and expect them to sell straight away. You need time in that market and moving your books in and out of Select will stop you from building readership on the other platforms. I have seen the compound effect on my blog, my online platform and my book sales over the years.

"It can take years to build readership at a retailer. Authors who cycle their books in and out of KDP Select will have a more difficult time building readership at Amazon's competitors."

Mark Coker, Smashwords.com

Independence and possibility of disruption.

I love Amazon. I'm a successful indie author because of the

changes they introduced to publishing, and I'm a happy Amazon Prime customer. But I'm an *independent* author, and I don't like being dependent on any single income stream because of a previous experience of this kind of dependence.

In early 2008, I was laid off along with four hundred other people in one day from my corporate department. My one source of income disappeared very fast. Few people saw the Global Financial Crisis coming, and we all had to adapt. Change is inevitable, so I choose to spread my bets amongst the retailers as well as selling directly from my own site.

In an interview with Charlie Rose in 2013, Jeff Bezos said that at some point, Amazon itself would be disrupted. He just hopes it happens after he's dead! I think about the future of publishing a great deal. I'm in my forties, and I'm not just building for the next year, I'm building for the rest of my life and hopefully leaving something for my family when I'm gone. As Amazon continues to rise and rise, we see the push back of many different industries against their domination. Who knows what the next five years will hold?

Dependence on one retailer with the power to change the rules.

Some authors have done very well from KU, and some continue to make fantastic revenue from it. But others have seen their income decimated when the rules around KU page reads or categories changed. Ultimately, you have no control over how much you are paid, and Amazon can change the rules at any time. They have done already, and they will continue to do so, because it's their business and they can do what they like.

Make your decision per book based on your personal situation

One of the best things about being an indie is personal choice, but of course, this can make it harder as well. I can't tell you what to do regarding exclusivity, but these are my recommendations.

If you have fewer than three books in a series or aimed at the same market, exclusivity seems to be the best way to go, at least in the initial period. I use KDP Select for my stand-alone books and my sweet romance pen-name.

When you have an established series that you are building over time, using more than one site is my personal choice. The compound effect will mean that over time, as I add books onto the platforms, and reach readers one by one, my sales will grow on the other sites. I also like spreading my income streams, so I am not dependent on one platform for my livelihood.

The more books you have, the more you can play with different options.

When you have multiple books, you can adopt multiple strategies. So writing more books in different series for different readers is the ideal situation and then you can have some in Select and some wide. The best of both worlds!

For more detail on success going wide, check out *Wide for the Win: Strategies to Sell Globally via Multiple Platforms and Forge Your Own Path to Success* by Mark Leslie Lefebvre.

2.7 Pricing and the use of free

"Customers care about price only when they have nothing else to care about."

Seth Godin

Pricing is most definitely a marketing tool, and if you self-publish, you have control over your book's price, and you can change it at any time. If you have a traditional publisher, then this is not your decision, but you should at least know the basics so you can understand the merits of various price points.

The sales price of your self-published print book will be based on the cost of production plus the margin for the print-on-demand company plus the profit you add. The only thing you can vary is your profit, so print pricing is not as flexible as ebook pricing. Therefore most self-published authors will just set and forget their print price because it can't easily be discounted. I usually add $2 profit per book onto the calculated cost to print.

However, self-published authors have an advantage over traditional publishing with ebook pricing, as we have the ability to change prices in a nimble manner, unlike traditional publishers who tend to leave the price alone as they have so many books to manage. Also, our overheads are lower, and we receive a higher royalty per sale, so we can afford to have lower prices. Here are some considerations for ebook pricing.

Use US$2.99 - US$9.99 for 70% royalty

Amazon has a royalty structure of 70% on $2.99-$9.99 for specific markets and 35% for *under* $2.99 or *over* $9.99. So for a $2.99 ebook, your 70% royalty is $2.05, and for $4.99 it is $3.45. Kobo and Apple Books also have 70% royalty, but no price constraints, so you can price outside those boundaries and still get the 70%. This is useful for higher-priced boxsets used for income rather than for marketing purposes.

Different categories have different price expectations

Non-fiction books usually sell for higher prices than fiction, as people are paying for information and an answer to a specific question. Fiction readers are often buying books every day or several per week, so they expect a lower price, whereas non-fiction readers expect the book to be more useful for the longer term. They might also read it more than once. My non-fiction also sells a lot more print and audiobooks than my fiction, and some readers say they own my non-fiction in ebook, print *and* audio editions. Check the Top 100 books in your category and see what prices they are selling at to see where yours might fit.

Use print book pricing to make your ebook look like a better deal

Ebooks should be cheaper than print books. It makes logical sense, readers expect this, and it makes the ebook look like a great deal if you have a higher-priced print product next to it. On Amazon, it will say how much cheaper the ebook is than the print, saving the customer a certain amount, so it's worthwhile doing a print book even just to make your ebook look even better.

How free can sell books

New authors often have an issue with free books, because they feel that in some way it undervalues the amount of work put in over months or years. But try to think of it from the reader's perspective. It's a risk to try a new author when it's so much easier to pick up the next James Patterson, so how can you entice a reader to try your book?

Think about the supermarket on a Friday night when they hand out samples of cheese or wine. You taste a little bit for free and then perhaps end up buying a packet of the cheese and a bottle of the wine. The large number of free tasters result in enough sales that the free promotion is worth it. It's known as a loss leader in the retail industry, something that gets a customer in the door and makes a small loss, in order to make a profit with other products.

It's a similar idea with free books.

If you're just starting out, then making your book free can help get your book into readers' hands and will result in more reviews.

"Don't offer a discount to get someone to buy your book. You offer the discount as part of a marketing plan that should have an impact on your entire business."

Kristine Kathryn Rusch, *Discoverability*

Free works best with the first book in a series

Check out my book, *Stone of Fire*, which is a permanently-free, or perma-free, first in series. It has over 500 reviews with a 4.1 star average, and there are nine books in the

ARKANE series. You can see from the 'Customers who bought this also bought' section that those who read the first book often go on to buy the other books, which are priced at US$2.99 for the novellas and US$4.99 for the full-length novels. BookBub reports that 60% of readers who download and enjoy free books by an author will go on to purchase other books by that author. So free is a discovery engine that will help readers find your books.

How do you make your ebook free?

If you're in Amazon KDP Select, you can set your book to free for five days for each 90 day period. All the other sites allow you to set the price to free anytime. If you want to have a perma-free book on Amazon, then set your price to free on the other large stores – Kobo, Apple Books and Nook – then report the lower price on your Amazon book page. You might have to do this several times, but eventually, Amazon will price match to free.

Some people consider free to be over-used and claim that the people who download the books for free often won't read them anyway and are being 'trained' to get free books. So there are opinions either way, but if you have no other way of marketing, changing your pricing and using free strategically can be a good start.

Price pulsing for promotional sales

Price pulsing is the use of limited-time price changes for a specific sales period. You lower your prices for a short time and promote the sale. Then, you can take advantage of the higher visibility when your price is back up again.

Promotional sales are a normal part of the retail environment. Customers expect to be able to get special deals on any product, and books are no different. If you do a promotional sale, you can expect to have more downloads of your ebook, exposure to a new audience, higher rankings and even placement on a bestseller list like the USA Today, as well as sell-through on books in your series or under your author name, plus exposure for your author brand.

It's a good idea to pay for promotion sites around a sale period, covered in more detail in Part 3.

You can schedule price changes for Kobo and Apple Books, which is great as you can just set and forget, but you have to change them manually for Amazon, Draft2Digital and other sites. Make sure you do this a few days earlier than your sale date, as the price change can take a while to go through, then remember to change it back again later.

If your book isn't selling, check the price points in your category

I had one author ask why his debut novel wasn't selling, and when I checked his sales page, the ebook was priced at $11.99. It was his first novel, and he had nothing else for sale. It was very unlikely that he would sell many copies at that price, since even the top sellers in his niche were selling for under $8. Look in your category at what other books are selling for. What is your market happy to pay for this type of book? Are you an unknown author at this point? If yes, play with pricing and other promotions to get the book moving.

Tiered pricing and higher-priced products

Having multiple books at multiple price points is a great way to spread your risk and offer a way into your books.

Many authors will price short fiction at 99c, novellas or short non-fiction at $2.99 and then longer works at $4.99-$5.99 upwards. You can use bundling to create value packs at higher prices as covered in the next chapter. The more books you have, the more you can play with pricing.

2.8 Using box-sets and bundling

Traditional publishers have always made box-sets for print books, and over the last few years, box-sets have become popular for ebook bundling too. They are great value for customers and often rise high in the bestseller lists, boosted by BookBub and other promotions.

They can be a great opportunity for authors to collaborate to reach a wider audience, or generate more revenue from one sale with their own series or themed box-set.

Ebook box-sets are a real advantage for indie authors, but many authors haven't started using them yet, so here's why box-sets are so great and how you can create them yourself.

What are ebook box-sets or bundles?

The ebook box-set or bundle is one file containing multiple books, so there is only one purchase and download for the customer. A boxset is not an anthology, which is usually a curated set of short stories or novellas on a specific topic, most of which will not have been published before, with a themed introduction to each.

There are a few different types of ebook box-set/bundle scenarios:

- **Single author box-set** containing multiple books in one series, priced at a discount compared to buying the individual books but still providing a good income for the author. For example, I have three-book box-sets for my ARKANE series and my London Crime Thriller trilogy, as well as a higher-priced nine-book boxset. These can be reduced for merchandising opportunities at Apple Books and Kobo in particular.

- **Single author box-set** containing starter books from multiple series as an introduction to the author's work. Many authors give these away as a Starter Library in exchange for an email list signup, but some also sell them as a taster.

- **Multi-author box-set** sold at a massive discount in order to hit the New York Times or USA Today lists. For example, I was part of The Deadly Dozen, a 12 book boxset for 99c which hit both lists in March 2014.

- **Multi-author box-set** sold at a good price for income purposes at a site like StoryBundle.com which bypasses the main retail stores in order to provide higher income for the authors and give money to charity.

Why create an ebook box-set?

Box-sets represent **amazing value for customers**, as they get multiple books for a lower price, which is why they are so popular.

Binge consumption has become more common, with Netflix customers wanting whole series of TV shows, and book buyers wanting enough content to last more than a few hours. A box-set satisfies binge readers and they also end up remembering you because they've spent so much time with your words. As Kristine Kathryn Rusch says, "The best way to get noticed is by publishing enough that readers can binge for a weekend."

Boxsets are **easier to merchandize** than single books because of discounting, and also a higher retail price means more income for the author and retailer. Kobo, Apple Books and other stores don't have a $9.99 cap on 70% royalty and in fact, the majority of my book sales income from those stores is boxsets.

You can get a **better return on paid advertising** like BookBub Ads or Facebook Ads for boxsets, as you need fewer conversions for a higher income.

You can sell boxsets for higher prices, so you get **more income per customer per transaction**, even though over-all the books are sold for less. You get more money up front rather than expecting the customer to buy all the books individually, which they might not do.

You already have the books available, so **why not add another stream of income?** Readers who buy boxsets are often a different sub-set to those who buy individual books, so why not appeal to both? You're leaving money on the table if you're not doing box-sets, especially if you're selling wide on Kobo and Apple Books.

Pricing decisions

Pricing for box-sets will depend on your intent:

If you want to **make income** for the longer term, then you'll want to price at a discount compared to buying the books separately but still at a high enough price to make it worthwhile for you. For example, my nine-book box-set at Kobo is $19.99.

If you want to **boost ranking** and have a massive number of downloads, or you're aiming for the NY Times or USA Today lists, then put as many books in the boxset as pos-sible and price low. Or start with a high price and then do a limited-time sale.

How to make your own single author box-set

As a single author, it's pretty easy.

Use Vellum to **compile the books together** into one file. It's super easy to drag and drop book files in. There are many other book formatting options, but Vellum makes everything much easier! Check it out at www.TheCreativePenn.com/vellum

Hire a graphic designer or cover designer to **make a box-set cover**. Get a 3D and a flat version, since Apple Books only accepts the flat version and Kobo recommends the flat version for better sales, so it's good to have both.

Decide on the price and then publish in the same way you would usually.

How to make a multi-author box-set

If you want to do a boxset with multiple authors, you need to make things a bit more formal. Consider the following aspects.

Do you share a similar audience? Genre box-sets do well, and they are used less often in non-fiction and literary markets, so that might be an opportunity for you. Regardless of what you're writing, consider which authors your books crossover with and work with them.

Rights and money. Whose publishing account will the box-set be loaded onto, who will get the royalty income and who will be in charge of all the money? You'll need to pay for promotions and potentially other marketing, so make sure everyone knows what's involved. These are the same issues faced with co-writing, which I cover in *Co-Writing A Book: Collaboration and Co-creation for Writers*.

You can curate and manage boxsets using Draft2Digital.com or BundleRabbit.com which also split the payments between the collaborators, so that could be an option rather than using one person to do the publishing work.

How will you split the promotion fairly? You need to divide the work between the group and keep communication simple and easy. Stay in touch and make sure everyone knows what is happening on which days. A highly coordinated promotional campaign will be needed if your aim is to hit any lists. A central shared Google Doc is a good start.

Clearly, a multi-author box-set is more complicated, but why not get started on a single author box-set if you have three books in a series or that are linked in some way?

2.9 Writing a series

"The more product you have on the market, the greater the chance that readers will find you. It's the simplest way to market your work and the one most suited to writers."

Kristine Kathryn Rusch. *Discoverability*

Writing a series, or books aimed at a similar audience is one of the smartest things you can do to market your books.

Repeat customers are much easier to reach than new customers.

A survey carried out by International Thriller Writers (ITW) found that readers tended to search for books by a specific author that they knew when they wanted to buy a new book. It also takes between three and four books for a reader to remember the name of an author and become a fan, so if you have a series (and even a three-book boxset), you are more likely to be remembered next time. As anecdotal evidence, I pre-order books from a few of my favorite authors because I'm a fan of a particular series.

The rise of **binge consumption** on Netflix and online streaming means that people want longer entertainment experiences. Some readers will not even commit to a new series unless there are multiple books available so they can immerse themselves.

Series make more money for authors.

Mark Coker reported in the Smashwords 2016 Survey that "when we compared the average sales of the top 1,000 bestselling series books against the sales of the top 1,000 stand-alones, the series books had 195% higher earnings and their median earnings increase was an impressive 127%. Readers love series!"

It's faster to write books in a series.

For fiction, you know the characters and the world, so you just need a new plot. For non-fiction, you know your target market, and what they need, so you can write more books to suit them.

You can use **branded covers** to create a look and feel for your series. This can also make book cover design more cost effective, as the title and images need changing for each book, but the overall design will stay the same.

All the online stores **use Series fields to link books to-gether** in a series. This means if a reader buys one in the series, they will likely get recommendations for the other books in the series. **Series can be used for non-fiction,** too. Just link books for a similar audience together using the series field. For example, this book is part of my series Books for Writers.

When a new book in the series comes out, you can do **price promotions on the first book in the series**, or make it perma-free in order to drive traffic every day. You can also use a pre-order to get early sales for the book.

This section has covered some of the prerequisites you need to have in place before you start with other marketing activities. Next, we'll get into short-term marketing.

Part 3:
No Platform
Needed: Short-
Term Marketing

3.1 Why book reviews are important

Book reviews are important because they feed into the book site algorithms. Think of them like a tally of check marks against your book, adding up to an overall impression. They also provide social proof to readers and can influence the decision over whether to buy. You also need reviews in order to be accepted by some of the paid promotional sites, so they are an important aspect to focus on.

There are three main types of review:

(a) **Customer reviews** on the book sales sites and Goodreads, posted by readers. These tend to be from your existing fans or people who like the genre and result in your overall star rating on the book sites.

(b) **Book blogger reviews** on specific book review sites that may bring new books to the attention of their readers.

(c) **Reviews in traditional media** like newspapers and magazines. These are dominated by traditionally published books. If you work with a publicist or pitch journalists, you're better off pitching a newsworthy story than your book. More on that in Part 4.

In the next chapters, I'll go into detail on the first two options, but it's important to consider what not to do regarding reviews upfront.

The problem with paid reviews

In 2012 a scandal erupted around paid reviews and 'sock puppets' where some authors were found to have bought mass reviews from places like Fiverr, or created false identities and written reviews for their own books as well as negative reviews for competitor authors.

A lot of authors got very angry about this, and it tarnished the reputation of online reviews in general. Amazon reacted by removing a lot of reviews from the site based on some kind of mechanism meant to weed out these fakes. They did this for all the right reasons as a customer-focused company, and these types of review purges have continued, but often they can sweep away 'real' reviews as well. They use a sledgehammer to crack a nut of a problem.

In 2016, the Amazon review policy was made even more stringent. Reviewers have to have spent at least $50 on the account they are reviewing from, a decision made in order to combat sites that were creating mass reviews under throwaway profiles. The policy also says, "posting content regarding your (or your relative's, close friend's, business associate's, or employer's) products or services" is not allowed, and neither is "Creating, modifying, or posting content in exchange for compensation of any kind (including free or discounted products) or on behalf of anyone else."

This essentially means that you can't ask friends, family and other people who know you to post reviews and you can't offer a free book *in exchange* for a review.

The purchase of Goodreads and also the use of star-only reviews within Kindle devices may go some way to combating the review issues over time. The main things to remember are:

- Don't pay anyone to create mass reviews on your book page on any site

- Don't create false personalities online and write reviews of your own books

- Don't ask friends and family and people directly connected to you for reviews

Most of us maintain our integrity when it comes to reviews, and it is still absolutely good business practice to give books away and ask readers to write a review if they enjoyed the book. These Advanced Review Copies (ARCs) are common in traditional publishing and remain an acceptable practice in the industry.

You can also submit your book to review sites that might be interested, get blurbs from authors in your genre, and consider reviews from 'official' paid sites like Kirkus Reviews or Publishers Weekly. These reviews have to be included in your Editorial Description on your book pages on Amazon, so they don't go into your overall review score.

Don't respond to bad reviews

It's inevitable. You *will* get one-star reviews from people who hated your book or just didn't get it at all.

Don't comment on negative reviews, and sometimes it's best just to avoid commenting on blog reviews of your books in general. People have their opinions, and you have to respect that. Authors who have gone after reviewers have seen their reputations suffer as a result. However, you can ask Amazon to remove reviews that are damaging personally, or if they are not actual reviews e.g. "I haven't read it yet," which is surprisingly common.

A one-star review can also be valuable as it shows what people don't like about the book. For example, one of my reviews for *Stone of Fire* gave the book one-star as it wasn't Christian enough. Although the book is based on Christian ideas, myth and history, it is not a Christian book, so that helps turn readers away who might not have enjoyed it anyway.

3.2 How to get customer reviews

If you're just starting out, and you have no audience, no email list and no fans, then you have a few options to get initial reviews on your book:

- **Put your book free**. Free books get a lot more downloads and therefore are more likely to get read and reviewed. You could also pay for a free book promotion on one of the many sites to get your free book noticed

- Pitch your book to **book bloggers** in your niche, as covered in the next chapter

- Use **Goodreads giveaways** to get your book onto people's To Read lists and ask those who win your giveaways for a review

- Make sure you **include a call to action** at the back of your book which thanks the reader and asks them to leave a review. This could be something as simple as,

    "Thanks for reading! If you loved the book and have a moment to spare, I would really appreciate a short review as this helps new readers find my books."

This will hopefully start a little trickle of reviews from your readers and will add up over time. You can also include a link to sign up for your email list, which I'll cover later in Part 4.

If you have an audience and a fan base already, then this is where your email list comes in handy, because you can use it to start building a review team, sometimes called a **Street Team**. This is a sub-set of your main email list, a group of fans who buy and review your books and are keen to help on launch.

I have *PennFriends* for my fiction, and before each book launch, I email my main list and ask if people want to join, so I am constantly adding new people to the sub-set. Then I will email the PennFriends and ask them if they would like an Advanced Review Copy (ARC) in ebook format. If they want to review that free copy on launch, I ask them to include a line: "I received an Advanced Reader Copy of the book from the author, and this review is my own opinion." This makes it clear to Amazon that this is an ARC review, which is a common and accepted practice in the traditional publishing industry, but there was no exchange required.

Once the book is available, I email the PennFriends to remind them where they should post the review. Generally, about one third respond with a review, most of them four or five stars.

3.3 How to get reviews from book bloggers

Book bloggers are readers who post reviews on their blogs, Goodreads and in Facebook Groups, as well as posting pictures on Instagram and other social media. They may even post videos if they are BookTubers. Reviewers usually read and review within a specific genre and may have a large audience of readers who take their opinions and recommendations seriously.

There are a lot of book bloggers out there, with more arriving every day and many others closing the doors and moving on. When you're searching for appropriate ones to pitch, make sure you check whether a site is still active by checking the dates of their latest post. You can also get an indication of their audience size by checking how old the site is, as well as how many social media followers they have and the interaction of their community. You want to make sure that you are pitching sites that have a decent-sized audience, although if you're just starting out, then maybe finding bloggers who are just starting out as well is also a good idea.

How to find book reviewers

Use your **list of comparison books** and authors to search for 'book reviews' or 'book blogger.' For example, 'James Rollins Seventh Plague + book blogger' would work for my ARKANE thrillers

Search **Facebook** for genre based book club groups and book review sites. Some welcome authors as members. Others are more private, so it's best to research the people who run the site before pitching your book.

Search **Instagram** using #bookstagram, but only pitch these bloggers if you have a beautiful cover that they will want to share

Search **YouTube** for BookTubers, video bloggers who share videos about the books they're reading. You can also check Twitter @BookTuber.

Use the Reedsy list of book bloggers at:

www.TheCreativePenn.com/reedsybookbloggers

Search **directories** like BookBloggerList.com, TheIndieView.com or BookReviewDirectory.com

There are companies that do **book blog tours**, but they are of variable quality. Some use the same blogs over and over again and there is little differentiation between launches. Others will tailor a blog tour to your book. Get recommendations or testimonials from other authors to check how effective the service is.

Go to **genre events and conventions**. Book bloggers are fans of authors and will often be at events, so you can meet some in person and make friends before pitching.

Use a premium service like **NetGalley**, which has a huge number of reviewers but does cost money to setup and the readers prefer advance copies so you'll need to be organized. They are also used to receiving traditionally published books so make sure your quality is high.

Check the data on publicly available reviews on your comparison titles. Go to the reviews on your comparison books, then click on the name of the book reviewer which will often give you a website and/or email address.

You can also use an automatic tool for this type of analysis if you'd rather spend a little money than spend the time doing it manually. Try Author Marketing Club's Reviewer

Grabber Tool, included in the Premium option at: www.
TheCreativePenn.com/amc

How to approach book reviewers

Don't use a scattergun approach to book bloggers.
Specifically target those who read your type of book. It's
better to pitch ten targeted reviewers than send an email
blast to thousands who won't be relevant.

Be respectful of their time and always **check their guidelines**. For example, there is no point in pitching your sweet
romance to a blogger who reviews scientific non-fiction,
and vice versa. Some bloggers might read ebooks, others
might want print. Some read indie books, others will only
accept traditionally published. Check first, and you won't
waste their time or yours.

When you email, **always use their name and make the
pitch personal**. Then say something like "I saw your
review of X by X, I have a book that is similar." Read their
About page and comment if you can, for example, I pitched
a blogger once who talked about their love of cats, and I
was able to weave that into the email.

**Include a short pitch for the book and your sales descrip-
tion**. You can also attach a nicely formatted document as
a flyer or include the book cover. Once they reply, you can
send the book in whatever format they request.

Don't follow up too soon, but do follow up. If the book
blogger doesn't give you a date by which they will post the
review, then follow up a couple of months later. But don't
be a pain or you might get blacklisted.

**Book bloggers are massively over-pitched, so you can't
guarantee a response.** Not all will post a review, and you
can't control the timing, so this isn't a launch technique

unless you do it way in advance. Most indie authors favor publishing as soon as a book is ready, but many reviewers work more to the traditional publishing model where they will get Advanced Review Copies before the book is launched, which makes it feel much more exclusive and special.

* * *

Pitching for book reviews can be a detailed and time-consuming task, especially at the beginning when you haven't built up relationships with bloggers in your niche. But it has been used to great effect by many authors, and traditional publishing still counts this as a huge part of their launch strategy, sending out hundreds of ARCs to generate buzz for a book. Indie authors can use this method effectively too. It just takes time to organize.

3.4 Paid advertising: Email blasts

"Good marketers realize marketing is not an expense, but an investment."

Seth Godin

If you have a financial budget for book marketing, you can use paid advertising to reach readers. Your sales will drop off unless you sustain advertising over time, but it can be very effective for selling books and also building your email list. This is usually a short-term tactic, so should be used in conjunction with other marketing,

You can also use paid advertising if you're just starting out, so you don't need to have spent years building an author platform to use it. I've found it effective for my sweet romance pen-name, which doesn't have a platform. You can also use it alongside other marketing tactics.

One way to move the needle quickly in terms of sales and ranking is to use paid promotional sites that have built email lists of avid readers who might be interested in your book. If you're combining this with a short-term promotional price drop, you can spike your sales.

Note: This is NOT the same as 'buying email lists,' which is a scam. Don't do that! With reputable services, you won't be given the email list, but your book will be sent out to those readers for you.

When should you consider paid email blasts?

This kind of promotion is worth it if you have a book with a **great cover and great reviews targeted to a specific popular genre**. The social proof of reviews is critical for people to trust the buying process, and you're unlikely to get accepted for paid promotional sites without them. The lists are also for the most popular genres, so there are no options for poetry and few for literary fiction, compared to the big sellers like romance, mystery or fantasy.

You also need to be able to reduce the price of your ebook easily and quickly for a short period. This means that you need access to the 'back end' of the publishing process, which generally means it's open to indie authors only, although some traditionally published authors can coordinate this with their publishers.

You must be able to afford a **budget for promotion**, as you may not make back what you spend and results do vary.

You can do this kind of paid promotion when you only have one book, but your results will be better when you have more than one. It's definitely worth putting the first in series on special offer in order to funnel people to the subsequent books.

What paid promotional sites are there?

There are a few heavy hitters that have been around for a while and consistently perform well for authors. These include BookBub, Freebooksy and BargainBooksy, Free Kindle Books and Tips, Kindle Nation Daily, and The Fussy Librarian.

But there are new sites and services springing up for authors every day, and others who close the doors, so the best thing to do is Google 'promote free Kindle book' or something similar, and then limit that search to one year, so you only get the most recent sites.

What is BookBub and how does it work?

The most effective email blast service is BookBub, which consistently moves the needle on giveaways and book sales.

BookBub.com is a free service for readers. Once you sign up, you get a daily email with curated books on special offer – either free or reduced for the categories you're interested in. I recommend you sign up as a reader in order to see how it works.

They also offer a premium promotional service to authors where you can advertise to their significant email lists through either a Featured Deal or Ads that go at the bottom of their emails. It can be pricey, but an author will usually get more than their money back in increased sales and visibility.

The Featured Deal listing is curated, so not all books are accepted, only the ones with good reviews and a discount that makes it a good deal for the reader. You can apply for international sites only, and it's easier to get these than the US deals.

Once you have a book out, you can claim your author profile at BookBub and build followers there – readers who might be interested in your deals. They also have a great book marketing blog with new articles every week including information from reader surveys and tips on how to optimize your paid ads. Check it out at insights.bookbub.com

How to evaluate advertising opportunities

There are plenty of paid advertising opportunities out there with more opportunities every day, but you have to look at some metrics to decide on whether to invest. Here are some criteria to consider:

- How targeted is the opportunity for your niche audience? For example, there's no point advertising a horror book on a romance website

- How much traffic does the site get and is it worth the money? Most sites with advertising will state how much traffic they have as well as rates for advertising.

- Can you get personal recommendations from other authors who have had success this way?

3.5 Paid advertising: Facebook, Amazon and other ads

"One out of every five page views in the
USA is on Facebook."

Gary Vaynerchuk. *Jab, Jab, Jab, Right Hook*

Twitter is my platform of choice for interacting with friends and readers, and I enjoy spending time there, but Facebook has become the power player in the social advertising market. I almost deleted my Facebook profile a few years back, but when they bought Oculus Rift and Mark Zuckerberg shared his vision for virtual reality spaces, I was convinced that Facebook would continue to be a big player even when social media marketing changes.

Then authors started reporting on how powerful Facebook advertising could be, so I gave it a try and revised my opinion on the platform. Now, Facebook Ads are an intrinsic part of my marketing strategy.

Times change, platforms develop, and everyone moves on. Even if you decide something isn't right for you now, then it might be later on. This is a good example of how I've changed my mind about a particular tool, and it's worth revisiting your assumptions over time, too.

All the social networking platforms have paid advertising options, and you should investigate the one that suits you best. In this chapter, I'll briefly outline how I use Facebook and Amazon Ads in particular, as well as my lessons learned from advertising. I won't be going into specific technical details because these platforms change all the time, but the principles remain. You can find specific courses or free tutorials if you want the technical steps. This is just an overview so you can investigate further by at least knowing what to look for.

Facebook paid advertising

I currently use Facebook Ads in a number of ways. When launching or promoting a book sale, I create **ads for the specific book** and target those to readers on my email list, people who like or interact with my Facebook author page and other people I target with comparison authors or keywords. **After sending out an email to my list**, I will also run an ad for the same thing – that might be a live event, a webinar, a book or a course. This nudge means that people see the offer multiple times and are more likely to click and buy.

I run **LeadGen ads** to build my email list by offering a free book to subscribers. LeadGen ads enable you to reach further than your current audience, and the customer only has to tap twice, rather than having to type in their email address, which makes it effective on mobile devices. I post articles on my Author pages and use the **Boost** feature to reach more of my audience, and I also use **retargeting**, which means running a second set of ads to people who interact with the first set, or with specific content.

One of the really useful things about Facebook is the ability to create **custom audiences** based on an email list you upload to the platform, or visitors to your website, or people who like or interact with your Facebook page. This integrates with content marketing, which we'll cover in chapter 4.8 and combines attraction marketing with paid promotion, especially useful if you write cross-genre like I do and you can't necessarily directly target specific reader groups.

You can also create **LookaLike audiences**, so if you upload your reader email list, you can then ask Facebook to find people who are similar to those people and then use that in combination with keywords to create a new target audience.

Importantly, Facebook does not keep or use those email addresses in any other way. They are protected by data privacy, but you should certainly have a privacy policy on your website detailing that you use cookies for tracking. There are lots of templates online that you can use to make your own.

Amazon Advertising

If you're new to paid ads, then I recommend you start with Amazon Ads because there are fewer choices, they are technically simpler and you won't accidentally break the bank. You can spend a few dollars and build up your confidence before trying other platforms. You do have to be the publisher of your book in order to use Amazon Ads, so they can't be used by traditionally published authors or those that have used an intermediary to publish on Amazon.

Login to kdp.amazon.com and you will find a Promote and Advertise button next to each book on your bookshelf. Click that and you will see the option to Run an Ad Campaign on specific country marketplaces.

You can see examples of ads by going to popular books in your genre. Underneath the 'Customers who bought this item also bought' area is another line of books marked 'Sponsored products related to this item.' Under the buy button, you may also see a single book advertised. These are Product Display ads. Of course, these options will change over time, so check the help documentation for details.

Amazon Ads are great because the image is always your book cover, so you have one less thing to think about. You just have to come up with the advertising text and the audience targeting, which can be keywords you choose or auto-targeted. I've found that auto-targeting only works with books that have built up an easily recognizable audience already, so it has worked for my non-fiction and sweet romance, but not my thrillers, as they are cross-genre. Chapter 2.4 gave you some ways to find keywords, and you can use the same tools to identify keywords for ads.

Amazon Ads give you an ACoS (Advertising Cost of Sales) score that enables you to easily see whether the ad is providing a positive return-on-investment. If it's under 70%, then the ad should be making you money. However, the ACoS score only relates to actual *purchases* on KDP and doesn't incorporate print books, audiobooks or KU borrows. As with Facebook Ads, you have to have some idea of your baseline sales and then see if your ads raise that baseline over time. But at least it's a good guideline, and if you're not into data analysis, it's better than nothing.

Promotions on the other book retail platforms

While Amazon has an algorithm-based system, the other ebook platforms rely on a merchandising team (yes, real people!) who recommend books for specific promotions. Kobo has a promotion submissions tab if you publish directly with Kobo Writing Life, some of which you can pay for, but in general, you need to have relationships with the vendors in order to get access to paid promotions. You will usually find representatives at writing and genre conferences, so make sure to introduce yourself, and demonstrate how professional your books are before you pitch for promotions.

You can use Facebook advertising to find readers on other stores, but it's definitely more difficult to reach these customers. I've had most success with advertising boxsets on these other platforms because the higher royalty offsets the cost of ads.

Lessons learned from paid ads

These principles should apply whichever platform you use.

Paid advertising is a normal part of any business. It's what you'd expect if you went with a traditional publisher, so if you're an indie, then you need to invest in it yourself. There are millions of books on the retail stores and your book won't miraculously be discovered unless you get some eyes on it. It takes a long time to build an author platform organically as I have done, and I should have invested in paid ads earlier. I've been overtaken by those authors who embraced it early and have used it to grow their book sales and author brand, so now I use it as a core part of my marketing strategy. Yes, it takes some time to up-skill, but it's well worth it if you are in this for the long term.

Create an eye-catching image.

For Facebook, I use canva.com and royalty-free images, or you can pay a designer on Fiverr or PeoplePerHour to design some for you. Some book cover designers will also include ads as part of their package. For Amazon, the ads use your book cover, which is why it's such an important marketing asset.

Set your budget and time-limit your ads.

It can be easy to over-spend on advertising, but all the platforms allow you to set daily or total limits on spending as well as limit the amount of time that ads run for. There are stories of people not capping their daily limit and then spending way more than they can afford. So start small and get your confidence up before you increase spend.

It will take **time and testing** to find a combination that works. If you set up one ad on one book with one image and one headline directed to one audience and it costs you $5, and you don't get a sale, this is not a total failure. It's just one failed test. When I advertise, I create several different images and different texts and use those to target different audiences. At the start, I might have ten different variations running, and then I turn off those that aren't doing so well and increase spend on the one that works, then monitor it in case it stops working. The best way to learn is by giving it a try, and you'll find you get the hang of it quite quickly.

Think more broadly about who your readers might be.

In chapter 2.1, prerequisites for success, I encouraged you to consider your target market and your comparison authors. This will come in handy for your ads too. For example, thriller readers who like James Rollins may also like my ARKANE novels, whereas readers of Tess Gerritsen are a better target for my London Crime Thriller series.

It's not just about direct return-on-investment (ROI).

Ask any marketer outside the author world, and they will not expect all ads to have an immediate ROI. For example, they would not expect to spend $5 and make $6 back every day. But many authors seem to think this is the expected result of ads and are disappointed when it doesn't pay off quickly. In Part 4, I'll go through how platform-building over time can result in long term sales, but the same principle applies to ads. Not many people buy from an unknown author the first time they see their book. It might take a couple of 'touches' before they purchase. An investment upfront to build your brand should pay off over time.

Ads are most cost effective when you have more than one book.

If you only have one book, then paid ads will likely leave you out of pocket. But if you have a series or a higher-priced boxset, then you can make a positive return across the whole of your back list. So you can pay to promote a free first in series if you know a certain percentage of readers will go on to buy more books.

Building your targeted email list is just as, or even more important, than sales.

This is easier on Facebook as you can specifically run ads to your email list sign up page, covered in more detail in chapter 4.7. You can also do it indirectly on Amazon by running ads to a free first in series that has an email sign up offer. Building your list means you have the ability to contact readers directly with your books over time and you can use that list to create audiences on the paid ad platforms.

* * *

Some authors are finding success with ads on Twitter, Instagram, YouTube, LinkedIn and Google as well as Facebook and Amazon. There are new ad platforms emerging, and the existing ones change their options all the time, so it's worth checking out new offerings as they appear.

You can find free tutorials as well as books on each platform, and if you want more detail, I recommend Mark Dawson's *Advertising for Authors* course: www.TheCreativePenn.com/ads

3.6 Case study: Ad stacking to hit the USA Today list

"Don't think in ads. Think in campaigns."

Steven Pressfield, *Nobody wants to read your sh*t*

So how can you use paid advertising to launch a book or rejuvenate sales?

In August 2016, my ARKANE thriller box-set hit the USA Today bestseller list at #121. This is a case study describing how I did it in case you want to try it yourself. But remember, this is only an anecdote, so results will depend on each individual's situation.

You can hit the lists with older books

A book is new to the reader who has just found it. This ARKANE boxset contains *Stone of Fire*, *Crypt of Bone* and *Ark of Blood*, published in 2011 and 2012, so they hit the USA Today list five years after publication. I hope that encourages you to always consider reinvigorating older books, especially those products that now have significant reviews. It's easier to get paid ads on older books because of the social proof in reviews they have gathered over time.

Why bother trying to hit the list anyway? What does it even matter?

In March 2017, Marie Force, one of the most successful indie romance authors posted on her blog that she would no longer seek to hit the top of the lists.

"No more chasing the lists. No more gaming the system. No more losing my mind trying to get the highest possible spot on lists that readers legitimately do not care about. Most of them wouldn't know where to find the lists online or in the papers. Chasing lists becomes an ego thing. It does not matter to readers. At all."

You don't need to hit a list to make a very good living as an author, and many authors just get on with reaching readers without caring about them at all. Authors who are in KDP Select may also be selling FAR more than is needed to hit the lists, but they require sales on multiple stores.

The lists are widely understood to be 'gameable,' so the results are more like an IQ test. They measure something – but not what you might think. However, there *are* a few reasons you might want to hit the USA Today or the New York Times list, or perhaps even the Amazon Charts, a new bestseller list announced in May 2017. Here's why I wanted it.

I was on the USA Today and New York Times lists back in 2014 as part of a multi-author boxset, and **I wanted to do it with a single author name**. Romance authors hit the lists all the time, even with brand new titles, but there are fewer indie thriller authors who hit the lists, so I wanted to see if I could do it. I don't like to constantly promote my fiction, so I needed some kind of spike promotion to aim for.

It's good to have a goal like making a list, and then even if you fall short, you still have the **benefits of visibility and sales**. I also wanted to investigate how fiction book marketing is working now in terms of paid advertising, so I used many of the promotional sites at the same time. All good research for this book!

What was the result?

I hit the list as I had intended and you can read the detailed breakdown of costs and revenue at:

www.TheCreativePenn.com/adstacking

As an overview, my book sales revenue was $4178, with over six thousand books sold across the platforms that week. The boxset also reached the Top 100 on Amazon. com and number one in five different categories. The total cost of advertising was $4965, resulting in an overall financial loss for the week of $787.

Even though there was a financial loss, that doesn't take into account the future revenue from the sale of other books based on new readers, which I would expect to more than offset those costs. Most companies would consider marketing as an investment and would not expect a positive return-on-investment from immediate sales in the week of the promotion.

Other measures of success included several thousand new signups to my email list, hundreds of Likes on my Facebook page and thousands of new readers who might go on to buy more books. The sales will also result in reviews and potentially word of mouth, plus the intangible social proof of hitting the list as a single author. So the promotion was definitely worth it for me.

Here are some tips on how you could try to hit the list yourself, if that is part of your definition of success. You can also use the same approach to maximise the impact of a BookBub ad, a free run on KDP Select or any time you want to boost sales on a book.

Make sure it's the right book and a good deal for customers

Established indie authors (mainly romance) hit the USA Today and even the NY Times with new releases all the time, but in the thriller genre, it is mainly traditionally published authors who do that. You also have to sell a decent volume across multiple stores to make the lists, so the best idea is to have a time-sensitive deal that people want so they buy on impulse. My ARKANE boxset contained three full-length thrillers: *Stone of Fire, Crypt of Bone, Ark of Blood*, reduced from $6.99 to 99c for a limited time, making it attractive to readers. There were 73 reviews at the time with a 4.9 star average on Amazon, which made it a good bet for the merchandizers.

Utilize ad stacking

I got a BookBub Featured Deal and then organized other promotional services around it for the week I was trying to hit the charts. I used Booksends, Just Kindle Books, Kindle Nation Daily, BooksButterfly, eReaderNewsToday, and BargainBooksy. You need to book these as soon as possible as many of them sell out early. They have varying success rates, but for the week of promotion I decided it was a good idea to be everywhere.

Draft2Digital helped me get some Nook merchandising, as you need sales in more than one store to make the USA Today or New York Times lists. As well as the paid email services, I ran Facebook Ads a few days before, so I would start the week at a higher ranking. On the Monday morning when the book sales started counting for the list, the boxset was already in the Top 100 for Men's Adventure and Terrorism, so it had a running start.

I continued to run Facebook Ads for the whole week to

fans of authors in the same genre, as well as to my email list and LookaLike lists. After the main BookBub Featured Deal, I used their beta ad service which shows paid ads at the bottom of the daily emails, to target Kindle and Nook readers for the final two days of the run.

I should have included tracking links per service in order to work out which was most effective, but I didn't because I'm just not enough of a data geek. My main approach was 'be everywhere' and then round up the numbers in total.

Use your email list in multiple ways

Your email list is a critical asset in your author business. It's like having your own BookBub but, of course, it takes time to grow. In the words of Gary Vaynerchuk, online marketing is about 'jab, jab, jab, right hook,' or 'give, give, give, ask.' So if you have been generous with your readers and fans over time, now's the time for the 'ask.' If you promote too often, then I don't believe readers will care too much, but if you only do deals occasionally (as I do), then you should get good buy-through.

I sent out an email to my J.F.Penn list notifying them of the deal, plus I mentioned it on The Creative Penn podcast and also sent an email to my Creative Penn list. Many people had already read the separate books, but supported me anyway with 99c, and some tried the book on a whim.

Readers often need to see a deal than once before they buy, so I also targeted my email list readers with Facebook Ads and used the list to create a LookaLike list of similar people to advertise to.

If this kind of paid advertising makes you feel negative in any way, consider these questions:

- Do you believe your book is good enough for readers to *want* to read it? Do you want them to know that it's available on special?

- Do you believe that your book will stand out from the crowd without readers being notified that it's on special?

- Do you think that publishers invest money in marketing for books they want people to read?

If you think your books are good enough and that readers will find them entertaining, useful or inspirational, if you take your author business seriously, and if you want to grow your readership, then I believe that this type of paid advertising investment is well worth it.

3.7 Algorithm hacking, big data and production speed

"It isn't about how many copies you sell.
It's who you sell those copies to."

Chris Fox. *Six Figure Author*

When one author shares information, it is anecdotal and nothing can really be gleaned from it other than interest. But if multiple authors see similar results based on testing hypotheses, then it's likely to be better information.

No one knows exactly how the Amazon algorithms work, in the same way that no one knows exactly how the Google search algorithms work. But authors have been making educated guesses based on sharing data points in private Facebook groups and KBoards and through sites like AuthorEarnings.com. Their findings have impacted book marketing trends, and this is likely to be an expanding area of focus over the coming years as AI and automation become ever more prevalent.

Big data and machine learning

You know those emails you get from Amazon that recommend books based on what you've previously read? Those are not handwritten by lots of Amazon workers sifting through virtual shelves; they are generated by an algorithm based on millions of data points about people's reading habits.

When you log on to Amazon you are shown different books than I am because we read and buy different things.

Amazon also uses machine learning and predictive analytics, so the algorithm is continuously learning and changing over time.

So what does that mean for authors?

Essentially, if you want Amazon to recommend your book to the right kind of readers, then you need to train the algorithm, so it understands who those readers are.

As Chris Fox says in *Six Figure Author*,

> "When we sold books to everyone we knew, we polluted our data. Amazon wasn't able to identify our audience, which is why our book didn't take off."

Of course, there are many reasons why a book doesn't take off, but this audience identification is a critical step. If all your family and close friends buy your book, the algorithm might see a sci-fi reader, a knitting pattern fan, a thriller reader, someone who buys children's books and an erotica reader in the audience for your literary fiction novel. How does it find more people like this to recommend your book to? And even if it does find people that match this profile, will they buy?

I took Chris's advice to heart when I launched a new sweet romance series co-written under a pen-name in spring 2017. I've spent nearly ten years building up an author platform, and I was desperate to tell people about the book as I wanted those initial sales. But with the algorithm in mind, I have kept the pen-name a secret and used Amazon Ads and Facebook Ads to target sweet romance readers in order to train the algorithm. I don't want to 'pollute' the data associated with those books with thriller or non-fiction readers, so I'm choosing to focus on attracting purely sweet romance.

So far, with no platform and no initial audience, I've had my best book sales month ever for a single book. So it's definitely worth thinking about.

30 / 60 / 90-day cliffs and production speed

All bookstores and retail shops cycle their inventory. If you have a print release, it may only be in the physical bookshop for a month, before someone else's book replaces yours in the queue.

In the same way, Amazon wants new content that it can recommend to voracious buyers. Readers will often browse the bestseller lists and hot new releases, and as a category reader, I will go to Thrillers and select those released in the last 30 days. As writers we know how many hours it takes to create a book, and as readers, we also know that it can take less than a day for a rabid fan to devour it and immediately demand another.

There's talk in the author forums about visible sales 'cliffs' or drops at the 30 day, 60 day and 90 day mark, and that the best way to combat this drop off is by publishing within these windows. A book every 90 days is ambitious, let alone one every 30 days – although Nora Roberts manages it – so most authors won't be able to do this in a sustainable manner.

Some authors are writing books in advance and then re-leasing them on this schedule, so basically writing three or more books in a series and not publishing them until they are all ready to go, then publishing them quickly to take advantage of the initial boost to keep momentum. This is a great strategy – if you have the patience!

For more detail on big data and algorithms, check out Chris Fox's book *Six Figure Author* or listen to an interview with him here: www.TheCreativePenn.com/chrisfox

Part 4: Your Author Platform. Long-Term Marketing

4.1 What is an author platform and why bother?

"Dig your well before you're thirsty."

Seth Godin

The phrase 'author platform' has become a catchphrase in the publishing and online business world. If you want an agent and a traditional publishing deal, you'll need to talk about it. If you self-publish, it will help your profile and sales online. If you have a small business, or you're a professional speaker, it will enhance your personal brand and expand your market.

Your platform encompasses how you can reach an audience of customers right now, or how you plan to do so in the future.

It is your influence, your ability to sell to your market. It is your multi-faceted book marketing machine! You might have a platform already.

- Do you have a popular blog or website that reaches thousands of people? Do you have an email list of readers who subscribe to your newsletter?

- Do you have a podcast audience? Do you have YouTube subscribers or followers on Twitter, Facebook, Instagram, Pinterest or another social network?

- Do you have a speaking platform? Can you get an audience to come and see you in person?

- Do you already have an existing business with clients and customers who might buy your book?

- Do you have other ways of reaching your target market?

Platform includes the actual number of people you can reach right now and the potential for growth over time, where you could potentially market, which includes your expanded network and connections. If you don't have any of this right now, don't worry. It takes time to build an author platform. We all have to start somewhere.

Here are some definitions of platform from publishing industry professionals:

"It's the way you, the author, will get your name and your book in front of potential consumers. It's the way you will bring sales to the table. It's a group of people who are likely to buy your book ... because they already know of you and they like something about you."

Rachelle Gardner, *Literary agent and blogger.*

"Platform is not ... about hard-selling ... annoying people ... being an extrovert ... Platform is not something you create overnight."

Jane Friedman, *author, publishing industry commentator and academic*

Do you need an author platform to sell books?

The short answer is no. You can absolutely sell books and make a good living without a platform, but you will need to focus on the strategies in Part 3. If you go that route, the book sales sites are your platform, and your books are content marketing in themselves. You will need at least an author website with book pages and an email list sign-up, but you don't need to blog, social network, podcast or build a bigger platform. If you just want to write and sell books, then write a lot for a specific target market, optimize your book sales pages, use paid ads, and see what happens.

But there are reasons why an author platform can be useful and worth building over time.

Attract an audience and a community

If you launch your first book and it sinks to the bottom of the charts without so much as a fizzle, then you will understand how important it is to have readers ready and waiting for your book. But it takes time to build an audience who want to hear from you, so your author platform represents the collective effort you spend attracting the right readers over years.

Grow a business beyond the book

Many authors think that they will hit the big time with their first release, but in reality, you're very unlikely to make a full-time income with just one book. Even with several books, it can be difficult, which is why most authors still have a day job. But you *can* make a good living with your words by building other streams of income around your books. An author-entrepreneur exploits the multiple opportunities and value in one manuscript and creates a viable business from the ideas in their head. How cool is that!

I am only a full-time author-entrepreneur because of my platform at TheCreativePenn.com. The site has led to speaking opportunities all over the world, as well as providing income from digital product sales, affiliate commission and book sales that enabled me to leave my job as a business consultant and become a full-time author-entrepreneur in 2011, and then for my husband to leave his job in 2015.

If you have a small business, or if you want one, then a platform can give you leverage online that can lead to a global reputation, global sales and opportunities beyond what you can even imagine right now. I cover the topic in more detail in my book, *How to Make a Living with your Writing*.

If you want to get a traditional publishing deal

A platform will help to prove that your books will sell, especially if you are writing non-fiction. Many agents and publishers will not even consider you if you don't already have a platform. Literary agent Rachelle Gardner says on her site that, "you really need to show that you are willing and able to put the time and effort into marketing yourself and building a readership online."

Thousands of books are published every month. Millions of blogs are available online. What makes you stand out from the pack? Why will people buy *your* book?

The bigger you grow your platform, the more opportunities will arise. If you have a professional-looking site with quality content, you can project a platform that will attract opportunity.

Network with a professional community

Professionals judge each other and socialize with other professionals they consider to be on a similar level to themselves. Your platform establishes you as an expert, someone who can add to the conversation. It can also foster great friendships that may result in promotional opportunities.

I have found this over the last ten years online as I've found a network of creative professionals. We understand the 'rules' in our niche, we do each other favors, we support each other and we all have something to lose. There is a level of trust and respect that comes from putting in years of hard work, and it takes time to earn.

Help other people and be useful

Many of us like to help others, and if you have a platform, you can do this more easily. That might be advice from your book or even advice about writing itself. It might be reviewing books or letting people guest post on your site. It can also involve supporting other authors' book launches, and in turn, other authors are more likely to help with yours.

It's fun, addictive and intrinsically rewarding

I love blogging, I love podcasting, I love Twitter.

Yes, I started because I 'had to' for marketing reasons, but now I wouldn't give those things up, even if I won the lottery, or had E.L.James's level of success. Creating and sharing is fun for me, and I have endless ideas of things I want to do, make and share. I'm a research junkie, so I want to share that with my fiction audience, and I'm a self-help addict, so I want to share all my tips from the author perspective on my podcast.

I didn't expect to enjoy all this, but I do. Although sometimes I've considered giving it all up to focus on purely writing books, I know I am more than an author. I'm also a blogger, podcaster, speaker, and entrepreneur. You don't have to be all these things, but I have become that person through building a platform online, and I love it!

Social karma and relationship serendipity

I don't know how else to put it, but I have gained huge benefits from building a platform that haven't been directly related to one tweet or one blog post or one podcast interview. Things just seem to happen over time.

An introduction to my first New York agent came from a relationship that started on Twitter and expanded into Skype chats. A Twitter exchange led to a podcast interview which led to being commissioned to write short stories for Kobo's Descent, a transmedia contest promoting the launch of Dan Brown's *Inferno*. My blog has led to me speaking at publishing industry conferences, which in turn has led to mainstream media opportunities, and there are many more examples. This serendipity only happens from putting yourself out there so opportunity can find you.

How much time does it take to build an author platform?

We all start with nothing.

No sales. No reader fanbase. No followers. No email list.

Building a platform is cumulative, but a little every day adds up over time. The trick is not to go into it looking for direct results within the first few weeks or months, but to enter with a spirit of service and generosity for your community and the people you hope to attract. Here's my journey from zero to platform.

In early 2008, I had one self-published non-fiction book and realized I need to sell it. I tried traditional media and made it onto national TV and radio, but it didn't sell any copies. So I decided to go online. I took courses about blogging and online marketing, and after two false starts, I finally settled on TheCreativePenn.com. I set up an email sign-up list and a very basic Author 2.0 Blueprint as a way to start getting sign-ups. My writing style was still stilted, impersonal and business-like. I hadn't found my voice.

In 2009, I started podcasting, but I didn't know much about it, so it was an incredibly amateur start. For my first interview, I put the handheld phone on speaker and held a voice recorder next to it! It was only later that I discovered recording through Skype. I also made some very amateur videos, all very serious, which are still available at YouTube.com/thecreativepenn. I started using Facebook and Twitter, experimenting with online tools and learning how to use them. I had very little traffic on my site, but I made a few connections to other new bloggers. I was reading a lot of books and doing courses and listening to audios on marketing. I also started writing my first novel.

In 2010, I joined the National Speakers Association in

Australia to expand into professional speaking. I started running workshops on what I learned about self-publishing and marketing. I continued blogging, podcasting, doing videos and social networking. By the time the blog had been running for two years, I was making some money and could see how the platform would scale. The building blocks were in place, so I repeated the same activities – blogging, podcasting, social networking, speaking, and connecting.

By September 2011, I had enough of an audience to leave my job and make a living online, albeit a small one at that stage. I continued to build on what I had started, adding to my content, products and books, essentially repeating the same activities within the same niche.

In October 2015, my husband quit his job to join the business and together, we run a multi-six-figure business – all based on my online platform.

Basically, I have done the same things for years. It's about consistency over time. Another brick in the wall each day! It's not a get rich quick scheme, but it can certainly be 'get rich slowly.'

My key learnings about building a platform

Try new things, invest in learning and make them a part of your life.

I love using video to connect with people now, but if I hadn't persisted, I would have given up back in 2009. I've also bought a lot of courses and books on how to use the various tools and techniques. But once you have chosen something, focus and get to grips with it before jumping into something new. Shiny object syndrome gets you nowhere.

Find what you enjoy and make it part of your life.

Much of what I do is no longer 'marketing' for me. I love the community on my blog, I love my friends on Twitter, I love interviewing people for my podcast. I started for marketing reasons, but I can honestly say that this is all part of my life now. It's the only sustainable way to do this long term.

It helps to use a smart phone. The best time to do a lot of platform building is in between other things. When I had a full-time job, I would chat on Twitter while getting a coffee, on a break between meetings or while waiting in line at the supermarket. I would read blogs on my commute and flag things that I wanted to learn. Now I use my iPhone for creating videos as well as posting pictures on Pinterest, Facebook or Twitter.

Be mindful of the time you spend on these activities. Track it and make sure that you are making the best use of your time. Make sure that you are creating more than you are consuming.

Use your platform to meet people and develop relationships.

I've made true friendships online as well as developing more casual relationships that have resulted in opportunities. Personal connection has always been the most important thing in business, and the Internet makes it easier for introvert authors! Be generous and promote others as much as possible. Remember social karma.

Don't give up.

It all takes time. Think in terms of the Olympic years. How

much can you achieve in a four-year period? Look back on your writing life and what happened in each of the Olympic years. For example, in Beijing 2008 I had one book, but I hadn't yet started The Creative Penn. By London 2012, I'd quit my job and was making some money, and by Rio 2016, the business was big enough that my husband had joined, too. I recommend reading *The Compound Effect* by Darren Hardy, which goes into how small, incremental actions can turn into something big after years of work.

Be grateful that no one is watching initially! It's brilliant if you have no traffic or no attention at first because then you can experiment and fail. By the time, people notice that you're around, you'll be fantastic!

It's totally worth it!

Content marketing and social networking have changed my life. I would still be a miserable business consultant without it. Yes, I've put in a lot of work, and if you work out my hourly rate for the first few years, it is abysmal! But I love this life and every month, more opportunities come my way because of the assets I'm building online. It's also a scalable income, so every book I write can go out and earn for me for the rest of my life. Compare that to working for an hourly rate that just disappears into the expense bucket, and it is the best time in history to be an author entrepreneur!

4.2 Your author brand

"Making promises and keeping them is a
good way to build a brand."

Seth Godin

If you have a book out already, or a website or a blog, or
you're a speaker, or you use social media, you have a brand
already. It's the impression that people get about you, the
feelings you evoke, the words associated with you. It's not a
logo, it's more about the way you are perceived. People will
form an opinion based on your book covers, your website,
your author photo, and how you use social media, but you
can control this if you consciously build a brand.

Your author brand is a promise to the reader.

It's about expectations. If your cover has two people cud-
dling and looking lovingly at each other as they walk along
a beach at sunset with the book title in pink curly font,
you'd better deliver a romance. If your website is dark with
brooding pictures and bloody handprints with articles
about the end of the world, you'd better not be selling
children's books. Everything you put out there under your
author name gives the reader an immediate impression of
whether they want to check you out further. The important
thing is taking control of what they see or hear.

You're reading a non-fiction book by Joanna Penn and if
you know my blog and podcast, you will (hopefully) have
formed an impression of me as positive and upbeat, focused on writing and publishing and useful on your author

journey. If I started using swear words and blogging about weight loss, or became snarky and critical, it wouldn't fit my brand or the expectations of my audience, and many people would leave and never come back to my site. It also wouldn't fit me as a person, which is why authenticity in a brand is so important for longevity.

My J.F.Penn brand is about fast-paced thrillers in fascinating settings, with an edge of the supernatural. You can expect to be entertained, and you can also expect quite a different experience to me as Joanna Penn. My book covers are different, my websites are different, and only about 5% of my Joanna Penn audience buys my fiction. Both are integral parts of me, but different people resonate more with one or the other of my brands. It would be confusing for a reader of one of my thrillers to come across this book. It just wouldn't fit with their impression of me, and most readers don't care about book marketing anyway.

These two brands have developed over time, so don't worry if you haven't got a clue about this stuff yet! You'll work it out as you keep writing.

Do you need to use multiple author brands?

Many authors write in different genres under the same name, and in fact, I originally published my fiction under Joanna Penn. But after a few books, I realized that my audience was different, and more importantly, my promise to the reader was different, so I decided to separate the two. I now write thrillers under J.F.Penn, I have different websites, email addresses, social media accounts and email lists. It is a lot of work, but in many ways, it makes my life a lot easier because I know who I am talking to and I know what works for each of those audiences. A different author name can also segment your audience and help train the algorithms about your target market, as covered in chapter 3.7.

You can use multiple author names on the bookstores and still only have one website, of course, but if you write children's fiction AND horror or erotica, then you'll definitely want two sites. But if you write thrillers and romance, you could probably get away with one brand.

Consider these questions:

- Who is my target audience for these books? How much do my audiences crossover by the types of book I write or want to write?

- Where do I want to be in five years' time? Can this brand grow with me? For example, your name will always last, whereas a site based on one book may not as you write more over time.

- Can I get away with just being one brand? What are the potential pitfalls if I do everything under one name?

How to design your brand

You need to actively consider how you want people to perceive you, whether that's through your website, your book covers, or your social media sharing. Consider these questions:

What words resonate with people who might like your books?

You have already started thinking about keywords and categories in Part 2 and this can be a starting point. For Joanna Penn, my keywords are writing, self-publishing, book marketing and creative entrepreneurship. For

J.F.Penn, they are supernatural thriller, conspiracy thriller (both categories on Amazon) and then things like ancient artifacts and manuscripts, religious history, international locations and good vs. evil. These words and phrases give an impression about what you can expect from these author brands.

What images will attract people who might like your books?

Your book covers need to resonate with the genre you write in, and the images you use will convey your brand. Kissing couples or dragons or massive robots in space or beautiful fonts can all convey an impression of the book inside. You should also consider branding your covers by series, so all books in the same series look the same in terms of layout and font, but with different images. Your readers should be able to spot your books immediately. Humans are great at pattern recognition, and you want them to recognize your pattern as they browse the stores.

What colors will you use for your website and social media?

If you compare my two websites, JFPenn.com and TheCreativePenn.com, you will see that I use different color palettes to immediately convey the difference between my brands. Darker colors imply darker themes and self-help sites are usually dominated by white space and bright images. You can see this in the branding of authors in specific genres – romance writers tend toward pastels, historical writers have old things featuring prominently, thriller and horror writers have a darker, edgier look.

For more ideas, check out your comparison authors in the same genre and see what they are doing for more ideas. Then give it a try!

How to build your brand

Once you have decided what you want your brand to be, you can communicate that through a consistent look and feel across your website, book covers, business cards/postcards, social media profiles and anywhere else you are public.

Be consistent.

Use the same photo across multiple social networks so that people recognize you. Put your face on your key marketing material if you can, because you want people to connect with you personally, not just your book. Use book covers that resonate across your author name and series. Try not to jump around too much with your brand ideas. Think about it, make a decision and then focus your energy on developing that brand consistently over time. The Internet compounds your efforts, so the longer you are in the game, the more effective you will be, whereas if you keep changing things, you'll have to start again.

Create content that resonates with your brand.

For example, on TheCreativePenn.com I won't talk about weight loss or scuba diving. I will stay within the boundaries of my brand because that's what readers and listeners expect (and want) from the site. That's why they keep coming back. I will also only tweet or share topics that fit with my brand on social media. At JFPenn.com, I share articles about ancient manuscripts or secret libraries or the occult in art and culture, all aspects that my fiction readers are interested in, but that wouldn't work on TheCreativePenn.

Find others to model in your niche.

Modeling successful authors is entirely accepted practice. Remember, it's modeling, not plagiarism! Look at what bigger names in your niche are doing and model your website after theirs. You can use their cover design as a starting point for what yours might look like, what colors you might want to use, what words resonate with that target market. You can model my website by using the tutorial at TheCreativePenn.com/authorwebsite

Branding is one of those topics that seems complicated, but you will work it out over time as you write more and discover who you want to reach with your books. Think about it as connection with people, not some corporate marketing term. Just get started, and you can adjust over time.

4.3 Using pseudonyms

Your author name is part of your brand, and the use of a pseudonym is something that many writers consider in their careers for different reasons.

(1) To differentiate brands and write in different genres

Many writers are prolific across different genres but to keep fans from being confused, authors use separate names, so readers know what they are getting. It is also useful because the online bookstores have separate author pages for different names, so books in particular genres can be grouped together. In an age of algorithms and machine learning, this can also separate your audience into more easily targeted groups.

You are reading a non-fiction book by Joanna Penn, and only a small sub-section of readers may go on to read my supernatural thrillers as J.F.Penn. I'm not hiding my identity, but I'm using a different name to make sure I meet reader expectations and to help the algorithms build a profile of my ideal reader.

More famous examples include Nora Roberts, who also writes as J.D. Robb; Ruth Rendell also wrote as Barbara Vine, Agatha Christie (whose real name was Agatha Mary Clarissa Miller) also wrote romances under Mary Westmacott; and Iain Banks also wrote as Iain M. Banks.

(2) To protect privacy

Many erotica and romance writers use pseudonyms because the nature of their writing means that they would rather keep their true identity secret. The same can also be true of memoir writers who may want to protect people in the book, particularly political or medical stories where litigation may be more likely. Author CJ Lyons uses a pseudonym because when she started writing thriller novels she was also a pediatrician, and didn't want her patients knowing about her alter ego.

When you publish under a pseudonym, you just use a different author name in the specific field on the publishing platforms. There are other fields for legal name and bank account name.

You can interact online under your pseudonym, and in fact, I have several author friends whose 'real' name I know, but I still call them by their pseudonym because that's how I think of them.

Many authors keep their identity secret, but of course, it is possible that you will be found out. E.L.James was identified as Erika Leonard after she made a gazillion dollars with *50 Shades of Grey*. But perhaps with that level of success, she doesn't mind!

(3) To disguise gender

Many authors writing in a male-dominated genre will use initials to disguise gender. Women read eclectically, but research shows that men will often choose to read books by men (even sub-consciously).

Some examples include Joanne Rowling writing as J.K.Rowling in the male-dominated fantasy genre, and later as Robert Galbraith in crime. George Eliot's real name was Mary Ann Evans, writing at a time when women weren't accepted as writers. I use J.F.Penn because action adventure thrillers are a male-dominated niche.

This also works the other way, and there are men writing as women in the romance genre. War veteran Bill Spence writes as Jessica Blair, and Lawrence Block writes under a number of both female and male pseudonyms.

(4) If the author's name is hard to remember or is unusual

Sometimes authors use a pseudonym that is easier to spell and remember. One of my favorite authors is James Rollins, whose real name is James Paul Czajkowski.

Other famous examples include vampire novelist Anne Rice whose real name is Howard Allen Frances O'Brien; Ayn Rand of *Atlas Shrugged*, was actually Alisa Zinovyevna Rosenbaum, and Joseph Conrad's real name was Jozef Teodor Konrad Korzeniowski.

(5) To publish faster

Indie authors these days publish as fast as they write, with no need to wait for a publisher's schedule. But traditional publishers have tended to only accept a novel a year from most authors, so many writers use different names to get around this restriction. For example, Stephen King used Richard Bachman, and Dean Koontz has admitted to using at least ten names.

* * *

Remember, there are no rules.

You can use whatever name you like, although it's worth checking whether someone else is already using it. Putting a middle initial in or using your middle name can also be effective.

4.4 Professional author photos

A professional author photo is a great marketing investment because you will use it on your website, book covers, social media profiles, business cards, speaking events, media mentions and more.

People make judgments based on their first impressions of our book covers, our websites and our online photos and avatars. They also judge us by what we blog about, our tweets, the photos we share, and how we interact with others. Everything you do that has your name on it relates to your brand. Your face is also part of your brand unless you're using a pseudonym.

Many authors resist getting a professional photo done, perhaps because most of us aren't entirely happy with the way we look. That's human nature. But it is *so* important to have a great author headshot as well as a way for people to feel you are a real person online. Your face is unique. People connect with faces, so share yours. The result is worth so much more than feeling self-conscious for an hour or two. You really have no excuse not to do this if you are taking your author profile seriously.

Preparation

Decide on what kind of photos you want and the location.

I had my photos done in Oxford, where I went to University and also the setting for some of my fiction. I wanted atmospheric shots for J.F.Penn and smiley Joanna Penn photos.

Research appropriate photographers.

Google "portrait photographer" and the place you live or want to have photos done. Look at their websites to get an idea of the type of pictures they take as well as their prices for your budget. You want to feel happy with how they do things and the results they get. I went with the lovely Mim Saxl, whose portrait shots are casual, yet professional, and I liked her attitude. You will need to email or phone your photographer to confirm times and dates as well as any other details.

Try on some different outfits. Plain colors work best for headshots as they don't draw attention away from the face. I had photos taken outside in May, which should have been warm, but this is England, so I took a jacket and, of course, it was absolutely freezing, so bring different clothing for weather options. Even if you're inside, take a few changes of clothes so that you can do different looking shots.

The photo shoot.

Look your best. Ladies, wear some makeup! If you're paying for pro photos then paying for some professional makeup and hair may also be a good idea. I didn't do pro hair and makeup this time, but I did practice beforehand and re-applied before the photoshoot. Make sure your look matches your brand.

Trust the photographer.

You have hired a pro for a reason. They will take lots of shots, maybe thousands, and many of them will be terrible. That's OK. They know what they are doing. Be sure to tell them what kind of image you want first, then trust them and let them guide you regarding location and positioning.

Imagine someone you love behind the lens for a more

personal look. You see some pictures of authors looking scared or just unhappy in their head shots, so try to be natural and move through some different expressions as the photographer clicks away. Keep imagining a real person smiling at you and smile back unless it's a moody shot. Anyone can tell a fake smile by looking at your eyes, so make sure that they are real smiles!

Tips from a professional photographer.

I asked Mim to provide some tips for authors on getting that perfect headshot. Here are her words:

Work somewhere with the photographer that has some special significance for what you like to write about.

For example, if your books feature famous landmarks, discuss incorporating recognizable features into the background of your headshot. You do not want an overly busy background, but it is still nice to get a suggestion of place in any shot – it makes it instantly more interesting. In addition to the interest in your shot, it will get you in the mood for being photographed as an author, and remind you of why you are doing the shoot. I suggest chatting with the photographer about possible locations and seeing what suggestions they have in response to information you give them about your work.

Wear something you love.

This is really important for anyone having a portrait done. You may think it is less so for authors, as generally, pictures of authors in books tend to be headshots, and so who cares what you wear, right?

Wrong.

Having your photo taken is a somewhat unnatural and potentially daunting situation, often involving posing. Most people don't like getting it done. Anything you can do to make yourself feel more relaxed and at home, especially if you're out on location with others around, is great. If you feel relaxed in what you're wearing, it will show on your face.

I also always recommend that people bring a couple of clothing options, so we can have a play and see what works best – and if you're working with me, stay away from busy patterns in clothing, they just distract from your face.

Choose your photographer carefully.

Look through the websites of a few in the area you want to work in, and see whose style you like. Are you looking for something more traditional and posed? Or maybe more modern, with shallow depth of field? Feel free to ring photographers for a chat. I have worked with lots of people who have had bad shoots with photographers when they just have not 'clicked.' A good photographer will put you at your ease straight away.

Something else to look out for when choosing a photographer is additional charges for using the photos – I choose to work by charging my fees upfront for the session, without additional fees for a DVD or use of the images afterwards – many do not.

Have fun!

A good photographer will help you relax and come up with some great shots, so sit back and enjoy the ride. And remember, they're probably nervous too!

Thanks to Mim Saxl, photographer at www.mimsaxl.com

What are you waiting for? Go and book a pro photographer now!

4.5 Integrity, authenticity, generosity, social karma

"Make stuff you love and talk about stuff you love,
and you'll attract people who love that kind of stuff.
It's that simple."

Austin Kleon, *Show Your Work*

One of the reasons we write for publication is for other people. We either want to help them through information or inspiration, or we want to entertain people and perhaps make them think. It can help if you consider marketing in the same way, because it focuses on the customer, not on you. This makes you think about what *they* want, stops you feeling self-conscious, will give you ideas as to what to share, and it will help you to connect with a community.

Generosity and social karma

The word karma implies that you get back what you give, and I believe this is true in the social environment. If you give, you will receive.

Being useful, helpful and generous is satisfying personally, but also builds up a bank of goodwill. When you later mention that you have a book out, or people are attracted to you because of your generosity, and see you have books/ products available, they are more likely to buy.

This isn't woo-woo. It's based on the science of influence. Read Robert Cialdini's book *Influence,* and you'll understand that the principle of reciprocity is one of the keys to influencing people's behavior. I believe that we can utilize such principles, but we don't have to do it in a scammy or unethical manner.

Co-opetition or collaboration with other authors

Co-opetition is about co-operating with your perceived competition so that both parties benefit. When there is a congruence of interests, co-operating together can create greater value than acting alone.

The self-publishing environment, in particular, is full of authors with an entrepreneurial spirit, sharing experiences openly. We discuss sales numbers and promote each other through blog posts, email lists and social networks, especially when our books are in the same genre.

In working and educating ourselves together, we can learn lessons faster, respond and adapt more quickly.

Traditionally published authors also do this through promoting each other's books, forming groups that speak together at festivals or doing book signings together.

For example, let's say you write science fiction. There's no need to see other science fiction writers as competition. Instead, think of them as potential collaborators on marketing projects. Both of you bring an interested group of readers who will read your books fast and be ready for the next book. If you collaborate with other writers in the same genre to promote each other, everyone benefits.

In the same way, non-fiction writers can work with authors in the same area to target the same readers. After all, a reader who buys one diet book will likely want to buy a whole load more of them!

Some practical ways of doing this include:

- **Promoting each other's books to your email lists** or including back blurbs at the end of your books. This can even go as far as producing collaborative books and bundles together.

- **Guest blogging** or interviewing each other in order to cross-pollinate readers. For example, I interview thriller, crime and dark fiction authors on my site JFPenn.com.

- **Creating genre-related sites** around multiple books of a similar genre that everybody promotes.

- **Sharing other authors' books or content** on social networks, and reviewing books in your genre on Goodreads.

If you do this type of thing consistently, without expecting a return, you will find the favor is repaid, sometimes from other sources and in surprising ways. That's social karma in action.

The importance of know, like and trust

"Be yourself. Everyone else is already taken."

Oscar Wilde

An important principle behind all of this is **authenticity.** Marketing from a personal perspective is about people getting to know, like and trust us. It's about delivering value and not just being about the sale.

Everything I do online is focused on these principles. For example, I might include a photo on my Twitter timeline of my desk, a sunflower from my garden or pictures from a research trip. This enables people to get to know me a little more without actively promoting specific books.

It's more personal but is also related to my books in a tangential way. Sharing like this is about building a relationship with people and allowing them a glimpse into your real life. If people know you, like you and trust you, they are more likely to want to buy your books.

Don't betray that trust once it has been built.

Think about authors that you love and who you trust to produce books you enjoy every time. Do you feel betrayed if they step outside the bounds of that relationship? Absolutely. So if you start to build a following, respect them and don't betray their trust. People come to expect what you give, so keep on giving it and they will continue to buy. I do believe that it is the author's right to choose what they write, but consider using a different variation on your name if it is wildly different to what you usually produce.

A great book on this principle is *Trust Agents: Using the Web to Build Influence, Improve Reputation and Earn Trust* by Chris Brogan and Julien Smith.

Authenticity and being yourself

"There no longer has to be a difference between who you are and what you do."

Gary Vaynerchuk. *Jab, Jab, Jab, Right Hook.*

The Internet is a marvelous place, full of creativity, generosity and amazing human endeavor. But it also has a dark side of scammers, dishonesty and trolls. I want to live in the former world, which is why I am fanatical about integrity and authenticity online. I share real stories about my life and real emotions, and they resonate with those people who want real connection. I find that being positive, upbeat, generous and creative leads to attracting similar people online. Yes, occasionally, I get haters, but I prefer to stay in the glass-90% full world.

How can you be authentic as part of your brand if you're using a pseudonym?

It's the same as writing authentic characters in fiction. You have to humanize them. You have to share personal details that make them a real person. I've done that by sharing articles, videos and audios about my journey as an author, the downs as well as the ups, and I don't hold back when I am scared or vulnerable – as long as what I'm sharing relates to writing! For my sweet romance pen-name, I'm sharing a picture a day on Facebook under an avatar profile. They are pictures that resonate with the novels but are also from my real life.

Decide on your boundaries

Of course, you still need to protect yourself and your family, and you need to draw the line you won't cross. Some authors happily share pictures of their children, others refer to them using code names and only share obliquely. You can still talk about details of your life without revealing too much. For example, talking about the challenges of writing while being a parent is a natural and authentic thing to discuss which also resonates with your brand as a writer.

4.6 Your author website

You need a home on the Internet, somewhere to point people to from the various social media sites, a hub for all the links to your books, products and events over time. Writing is a long-term career, and if you want to take this seriously as a business, you should own and control your own website, because only then can you guarantee longevity and security of the site over time.

Some authors build their author hub with a Facebook page or other social media site. But remember Myspace. The popularity of these websites change over time, and they also change the rules. If you use a free site or free hosting, you do not own the site or the content, and the company could go under or turn off that service at any point. Everything you've built may disappear unless you own, control, and backup your own site.

Your domain name and website set-up

Many first-time authors make the mistake of setting up a site around the book name or theme, without considering their longer-term career. It's best to buy the URL for your author name if you can, or use an initial or the word author after your name if that is already taken. If you use multiple brands, you can buy other URLs and redirect them to the same site at first and build separate sites over time.

This is not a technical book, but I have made a tutorial on how to build your own author website in under 30 minutes at:

www.TheCreativePenn.com/authorwebsite

I take you through how to set up a basic author website

without spending much money, and it includes the various sites I use for hosting and design. It's a good idea to keep it simple and learn the basics yourself so that you can change your design and content over time as you learn more skills. Many premium WordPress themes have SEO design, making it easy for search engines to find and index your site, as well as mobile-responsive frameworks so readers can find you on whatever device they are using.

Don't obsess over design until you have more of a clue about what you want to do with your author brand. My sites are almost unrecognizable since their first iterations, but the beauty of WordPress is that you can change the design and make it mobile compatible, while still retaining the underlying content. Build your site with a clean, easy-to-read and simple design and update later. After several redesigns over the last few years, I currently use the Genesis Beautiful Pro theme – but I know that this won't be the last time I update it!

We all start with nothing.

No traffic to our site. No sales.

No followers. No list.

That's just the way it is. Becoming a pro writer is a long-term project so don't worry if you have nothing now. It will grow over time, as will your profile as a writer if you keep building it consistently. I would be nowhere if I hadn't started with a terrible-looking site and tweaked it along the way. If you don't get started now, you may still have nothing this time next year.

What do you need on your author website?

Once you get your site up and running, start by setting up these basics:

A Home page with an introductory blurb about you and your books.

If people have come to your site via a link to a blog post, the Home or About page will likely be the next page they'll look at if they stay on your site. Visuals are critically important, especially 'above the fold,' so no one has to scroll to understand what's going on.

An About page.

This could be a more personal introduction as well as your official bio and could include a short version that can be swiped and used for interviews and introductions. Include your professional author photo if you're not writing under a pseudonym because people connect with people.

An email list sign-up for your updates and a free book offer if you have one.

More on this in the next section.

Book pages with buy buttons for all formats and all sites.

I have individual book pages as well as a main one from the menu bar on my sites, so the reader can always find details of the books and links to the appropriate stores. If you have a lot of books, then a list of the various books in order can be useful.

A contact page.

You need to have some way that people can connect with you. Set up an email account specifically for your author name. I use GSuite which provides email for websites, and I have different author emails per brand. You can also use a form on your Contact page, which will lessen the amount of mail you get. I use Gravity Forms.

Those are the main things you need, but you might also like to include:

A press page or media kit.

The phrase 'media kit' sounds pretty scary, like it's some complicated tool that only certain people understand. But actually, it's just a set of information that helps journalists and bloggers find what they need.

Add your contact details and your agent if you have one. Include phone numbers if you can, as journalists often want instant access; a short bio and long bio; professional pictures with headshots and action shots that can be used in media with photo credit details if necessary; a list of awards, endorsements, press coverage or media quotes if you have them; links to your books and cover images; sample interview questions, and a one-pager on each book.

Over time, you will be featured in various media, so collect those clips and use 'As featured in' on your home page as social proof. We are tribal creatures, and this social proof might make a difference to whether people will be interested in buying your books or giving you attention.

A page for book clubs.

Book club members are voracious readers who will devour a whole backlist and spread the word about books they like. You can make it easier for them to use your books by developing lists of questions or discussion points around your book. For example, my ARKANE series goes into questions of religion vs. science, faith vs. doubt. What are the themes of your books and how could you incorporate them into a framework for a book group?

An events and appearances page.

If you speak at literary events or do book signings or other events, list those on a specific page and include links for people to book them.

A blog.

You can have a blog as part of your website, but if you don't produce content for it regularly, then call it Articles or News or something other than Blog. I have a Blog link on TheCreativePenn, but an Articles link on JFPenn, as I don't post there so often. It's also not necessary to blog at all, covered in more detail in chapter 4.9.

Next steps

Once you have a home base on the Internet, you can direct everything else back to it.

- Update all your social media profiles

- Add your site to physical marketing materials like business cards and postcards

- Add your site to the back matter of your ebooks and include it on the back cover of print books

- Add it to your email signature

Remember to keep your website updated with new books over time because it's how readers, journalists, agents and publishers can always find you.

4.7 How to build an email list

Getting a BookBub featured deal can propel you into the top of the charts and be the basis of a campaign to hit bestseller lists. But what if you had your own BookBub, an email list of targeted readers who signed up on your site and were waiting to buy your next book?

It is possible.

Why build an email list?

Seth Godin, author of many marketing books, describes permission marketing as "the privilege (not the right) of delivering anticipated, personal and relevant messages to people who actually want to get them."

If you have your own email list of people who have given permission, you have a way to contact readers and fans when you have a new book out, and that gives you **more control over sales**. You can also build a sub-set of that list, people who read your book before launch and are ready with reviews when it goes on sale. Some authors even source beta readers from their email audience.

You can also **build up a relationship with readers** over time, so they get to know who you are. Remember the principles of know, like and trust? Well, email is a great way to communicate and is much more direct, targeted and relational than social media. I consider email to be a huge part of my direct 1:1 marketing efforts and spend a good part of every day answering email from readers and my community.

The power of your own email list is also about true independence, the ability to sell your books even if all the book sales websites disappeared. If you're traditionally published, it's the ability to walk away from a publisher without fear, because you know you have an audience you can reach yourself.

If you're on your first book, you may see building an email list as an insurmountable challenge. But if you start a list with book one, then you will have at least a handful of people to tell about book two. We all start with zero, and your list will grow over time as readers find you or if you actively promote it. The best time to start building an email list is right now, wherever you are on the author journey.

Here are some tips on how you can use email marketing with integrity.

Don't add people to your list manually

People should actively opt in by signing up themselves in exchange for something specific. You can activate double-opt-in on your list, which means people sign up and then click a Confirm link by email before they get emails. This is an anti-spam mechanism that helps to ensure permission.

Don't buy lists, either, because those people have not specifically asked for information from you. I get spam emails every day from people who have signed me up to lists with an email I never use for that type of thing. I delete and block them immediately.

Respect your list

Keep their details private. Don't sell or share your list with anyone else. Include a privacy policy on your website that explains how you will interact with them. There are lots of templates online that you can modify for your site. Be a valuable resource to your subscribers by providing information, inspiration or entertainment. You do not ever want to be seen as a spammer, so give away great information, offer quality on a regular basis for free, and people will be happy to buy from you when you have something they are interested in.

You have permission to email but only with information relating to what they signed up for

So if you sign up for my Author Blueprint at: TheCreativePenn.com/blueprint, I will only email about writing, publishing, book marketing and creative entrepreneurship. I won't start emailing about weight loss products. My emails to my fiction audience are completely different again.

Make it easy for people to unsubscribe

At the bottom of all good email services that comply with anti-spam laws is a way to unsubscribe automatically. You *want* people to unsubscribe if they are unhappy with what they are getting from you. Remember that your books are not for everyone! As your list grows, you'll also pay more for the service, so you only want people on the list who want to be there.

What will you offer in exchange for an email address?

Many authors have a sign-up for a newsletter on their website, but as a reader, do you want another newsletter? Do you need another email cluttering up your inbox? Think about what is useful, entertaining or inspirational for your target market. What would they really want?

For fiction authors just starting out, try using a short story or a novella based around one of your characters. If you have more books out, you can use a full-length book or even a bundle of books, for example, the first in each of your series. I give away an action adventure thriller novella at www.JFPenn.com/free

For non-fiction, you could give away a PDF of useful tips, excerpted chapters or one of your books. You could also give away free video training or audios. If you sign up for the Author Blueprint, you receive a free ebook as well as a number of video and email tutorials.

Of course, you can build up your offer over time. I started out with 'sign up for my newsletter' on my fiction site and a one-page PDF of tips for my non-fiction. But over the years, I have increased my offer. So just get started where you are, and you can change it up over time.

Note: You can't give away any books that are in KDP Select because they have to be exclusive to Amazon.

I use and highly recommend BookFunnel.com for delivering free books as part of the email list sign-up process. You can also use it for sending ARCs to your early readers, and they can watermark the ebooks in case you're concerned about piracy. They allow books to be delivered to any digital device and handle customer service for those technically challenged readers.

How to set up your list

The first step is to **sign up for a list management service,** because you can't just email people from your personal account. There are lots of options and authors often try several. I recommend ConvertKit for those starting out, because it's easy to use and there is a lot of help information. I use it for my sweet romance pen-name. You can check it out at www.TheCreativePenn.com/convert. I also have a tutorial at: www.TheCreativePenn.com/setup-email-list

Other recommended services include Mailchimp, Aweber, MailerLite, and Active Campaign, and there are more emerging all the time. Compare the various services to see what would suit you best.

Then **set up a sign-up form** using one of the templates from the email service. Once you've picked one and customized it, they will give you a little piece of code to copy and paste into your website. It will appear as a signup form that the readers can now use to enter their email and start the process of receiving messages from you. You can put it at the top of the page, on the sidebar, on its own special page, in a pop-up, or all of these at once. It's up to you.

You also need to **set up a series of emails for subscribers**, known as autoresponders because they go out automatically when someone signs up.

This might be as simple as one they receive straight away with your free offer, or you might have a whole sequence that guides them through a process. My Author 2.0 Blueprint autoresponder has a series of weekly emails describing how to write, publish and market books as well as make a living writing. These are useful for the reader but also enable them to get to know, like and trust me so they might be interested in buying a book or course at some point.

Each email list provider also provides a **Broadcast mechanism** to send newsletters or notification of sales, events or book launches. They have templates you can use so you can just drag and drop images in – no need for a complicated set-up anymore!

It's a good idea to test the sign-up form and emails by signing up with a test account and sending yourself a newsletter just to make sure that everything is OK. Then you're ready to go!

Add the list sign-up to the back of your books by listing the free giveaway and the URL.

When someone has just finished and loved your book, that's when you're in the most powerful position to ask them to join your list. If you are traditionally published, it's worth asking your publisher if you can include a link to your email list at the back of the book. Pitch it as being useful for connecting with readers and making marketing easier for the next book.

You can use a clickable link in ebooks, but use an easy to type URL in print books. It's also a good idea to have a URL that's easy to say out loud, as you can then mention it on podcasts, interviews and when speaking. Take any chance you can to give people an option to sign up!

Here's what I include at the end of my ARKANE novels:

* * *

Thanks for joining Morgan, Jake and the ARKANE team!
Enjoyed *End of Days*? Here's what you can do next.

If you loved the book and have a moment to spare,
I would really appreciate a short review. Your help in
spreading the word is gratefully received.

The next ARKANE adventure will be available in the coming months. Get your free thriller plus notification of the next book as well as giveaways and pre-release specials at: www.JFPenn.com/free

Remember, it will be a trickle at first, and your list will grow over time, just like everything else in the author business.

What do you include in your Broadcast emails?

Once you start building a list of email subscribers, you need to keep talking to them. Some authors get stressed over what they are meant to send, but this will differ depending on what you promised at sign-up and also what you are doing with your author business as a whole.

Non-fiction authors tend to use email marketing more regularly, because it is a major source of income through affiliate commission, consulting, or product sales, rather than just books. Most fiction authors have more sporadic updates that include some interesting research and life tidbits as well as upcoming releases.

You could include **news and articles** about your industry or niche; **your own articles, audio or video** which might include personal items like photos from your research trips; details about your **new book** or product releases; **book reviews** related to your niche; or **competitions,** giveaways and anything else relevant to your audience.

You want people to open your email, so make it interesting and **include a headline** that will make them want to read on. **You need to send emails regularly** enough so it is not a surprise when you do send one. Don't just email when you have something to sell. Build a relationship over time. Fans want to know what you're up to, and they will be interested in what you have to share with them.

But there are no rules!

The bare minimum is to simply have a list of people to notify when your next book comes out and then you can improve your communication over time. Remember, every name on that list is a person, so think about connecting with them on a personal level.

Build a Street Team

Some of the people on your email list will be super-fans who read all your books and love everything you do. They will be a small sub-set but they are the ones you want to engage with more regularly, so it's worth setting up what's known as a Street Team. This is a group within your main email list who get your Advanced Review Copies (ARCs) before official release and help you by reviewing the book or spreading the word on blogs or social media.

You can build this smaller sub-set by emailing the main list and asking them to apply. I do this before each launch, adding a few people every time to my PennFriends, and other authors include an email in their autoresponder series.

Use your email list in paid advertising

Your email list can be incredibly useful for paid advertising. You can load a list of emails into Facebook, and they will create an Audience who you can then advertise directly to. When I email my list about a new book, I will also do an ad to the list audience at the same time. Readers often need exposure multiple times before they buy.

You can also create a LookaLike audience, where Facebook will go and find other similar people who you can advertise to, attracting more people to your list over time. Your ads will likely be cheaper if you use your list and a LookaLike, so it's well worth incorporating this step into your marketing strategy.

Have email lists stopped working?

There has been a backlash against list-building in some parts of the author community, complaints that lists are not performing and that the expense of maintenance is not covered by sales at launch. If you're struggling with your email list, here are a few things to think about:

- Are you offering value to your readers? Are your emails interesting or entertaining? Are they worth opening? Do you provide more than just 'buy my book'?

- Are you *only* building your list through sites like Instafreebie or mass giveaways? Are you segmenting these free readers so you can see how they are different to people who find you through your books? Are you cleaning your list to remove those who only want free books and don't contribute with reviews?

- Are you keeping your list warm by communicating with them regularly?

- Are you building a Street Team, a subset of super fans who help with the launch?

Like any of the marketing methods, building and maintaining an email list takes time and effort, but it can be one of the most powerful aspects of a long-term author business.

4.8 Content marketing

"You can buy attention (advertising). You can beg for attention from the media (PR). You can bug people one at a time to get attention (sales). Or you can earn attention by creating something interesting and valuable and then publishing it online for free."

David Meerman Scott,
The New Rules of Marketing and PR

Content marketing is creating and sharing online material like articles, audio, video and images that don't explicitly market products but instead attract attention to your website or profile. Some of the people who check out that content may sign up to join your email list or follow you, and may eventually buy your books or products. It is an attraction form of marketing.

Content marketing for authors can also include flash fiction or short stories posted for free on your site or published in magazines that attract readers to you. It can also be chapters on Wattpad or other story-sharing sites, or a novella a month published on the book retailers. So your books themselves can be content marketing. Good news for writers!

What is the point of content marketing?

You may have noticed that the Internet is full of free information, inspiration and entertainment. That's what people generally go looking for when they search online. There are millions of sites that will give them what they want, and your book can be lost in the myriad of options.

Content marketing is one way to stand out in a crowded market.

Each piece of content you put out there is another way for people to find you. It's another breadcrumb that might lead someone to your book. By spreading your content across different media, you will be able to target a variety of audiences.

Provide good quality, useful or entertaining content which brings people to your site. They begin to know you, like you and trust you, and then when you have a book launch, they might consider buying your book. Thousands of books sink to the bottom of the sales charts every week because nobody knows they are there. How can you ensure your book isn't one of them?

Content marketing vs. social media

With content marketing, you create something original. This can be flash fiction or a short story, a blog post, video, podcast, or an ebook giveaway. You own it, and you host it somewhere that you can control.

This content lasts a long time and continues to be relevant. It can be found in search engines, and people may consume it or link back to it years later. For example, people who discover my podcast on iTunes often go back and listen to years of backlist interviews, because the content is evergreen.

Social media is mostly ephemeral content, designed to catch attention at the point when someone is present at that moment. Posts on Facebook, Twitter or Instagram and other social media only appear briefly on timelines and then sink in the mass of other things going on. Anything on social media is immediate and fades fast.

You don't own the platform, so posts on social media can disappear at any point. This is the main reason why you should never build your entire platform on someone else's online real estate, because when the rules change, your business will be impacted.

Some people put everything into Myspace, and then it sank with the rise of Facebook. Now people are doing the same with Facebook or Instagram. So, use the social media tools, but build the base of your platform on your own hosted site and use social media to drive traffic to your list.

Social media often includes links to content but is also about sharing other people's content, as well as discussions, comments and more interactive relationships.

You can use both in conjunction, but it is critical to build good quality, long-lasting, original content if you want to become known online. The rules are the same whether you're an author or someone with another type of online business.

So, what types of content can you produce?

Here are just a few examples but there is no limit to what you can produce.

(1) Text article or blog post

Blogging or writing articles helps to build your brand and attract an audience. You can also write guest posts on other blogs within your niche and aim to write for bigger sites with a wider audience. But blogging is a different type of writing to fiction or even non-fiction books, and not all blogging is content marketing. Compare these examples.

(A) You set up a personal blog for the purpose of sharing holiday photos. This is blogging but not content marketing. Or you talk about your writing life but never think about what your audience might be interested in.

(B) You write useful articles in a specific niche to attract a target market who might be interested your books, products or services. You are most definitely content marketing, as well as blogging.

(2) Video

Google owns YouTube, and video search is growing as streaming internet speeds improve, and people have shifted to online video for longer-form content. It's not just 30-second videos of LOLcats anymore! You can do interviews, talking head opinion pieces, funny skits, vlog chat shows, book trailers, on-location research videos and many more options. More on this in chapter 4.18.

(3) Audio

Podcasting has taken off in recent years due to the ease of downloading and listening on mobile devices. Podcasts are audio shows that people can subscribe to for free, distributed over the Internet through services like iTunes.

When people listen to your voice for thirty minutes to an hour every week, when they hear you laugh and talk about your books and writing life, they feel like they know you. Building trust and rapport is key to content marketing, and both audio and video are brilliant ways to do this. More on this in chapter 4.16.

(4) White paper, ebook, free report

My Author 2.0 Blueprint contains ideas that you can use to write, publish, sell and promote your book right away. It's free, and people sign up for it every day because it provides useful information. Fiction authors often use short stories or novellas, or even full books for giveaways.

(5) Teleseminar or webinar

You can do live events easily now using paid services like GoToWebinar as well as free options like Google Hangouts. When people listen to your expertise, ask questions and engage with you, it can result in immediate opportunities because you have a connection. Many Internet marketers now use this type of content to generate leads and product sales. Some even do online conferences with multiple speakers.

(6) Photos or images

Hugh Macleod from GapingVoid.com is known for his cartoons on the back of business cards which led to a multi-book deal on top of a successful Internet business. I highly recommend his book on creativity, *Ignore Everybody and 39 Other Keys to Creativity*. Hugh sends out illustrations to his list every week, which can be shared on social media, but he also has merchandize like T-shirts, books and prints, so his free content sells his business.

Images have also become hugely important in social media channels like Instagram and even text-based social media is now image-heavy. More on this in chapter 4.12.

You can also re-purpose your content, combining these options to reach a wider audience. So you can write a text article, then talk about it in a video or a podcast, include it in your email newsletter or create an infographic from it as well as sharing it on social media sites.

An example content marketing production schedule

I'm not someone who enjoys the hard sell, from either end of the experience, so I've embraced content marketing wholeheartedly because it enables me to attract people by being useful, inspirational or entertaining. This is my content production schedule which I have kept up since late 2008.

Every day, I post useful links to other sites and some of my own on Twitter @thecreativepenn as well as respond to @ comments and replies. I post one thing on my author Facebook pages and these days, I often post a picture on Instagram. There are a lot of social media scheduling tools, like BufferApp and MeetEdgar, so you don't have to be online every day. Most of my social media is scheduled in advance across multiple time zones.

Every 2-3 days, I post an article, video or audio podcast on The Creative Penn. I mostly batch the creation and have at least a week's worth prepared in advance. When I first started, I posted more often because I was trying to raise my ranking with Google, but these days, the schedule has slowed as the site is more well-known.

Every week, I post a video on YouTube and schedule an audio podcast with an interesting guest, plus add a transcript and show notes on the blog. The Creative Penn podcast has over 540 episodes and counting.

Every month, I appear on several podcasts as a guest, as well as doing a live event or webinar. I also post interesting articles at my fiction site, JFPenn.com, at least once a month.

Every year, I write and publish several books, across fiction and non-fiction and use some of the chapters as content marketing on the site.

It might look like a lot of work, but if you love what you're doing, you'll never run out of ideas!

4.9 Should you have an author blog?

Blogging changed my life.

Seriously.

Back in 2008, I had a non-fiction book but no one knew about it, and no one knew who I was. I had no author friends and thought that those kind of friendships were totally unattainable for me. I had only written journals and business documents. I didn't have a 'voice.' I didn't know what I wanted to do with my life, but I knew I was un-happy in my day job as a business consultant and I needed a change.

After a few false starts with traditional media promotion for my book, I discovered blogging, and at the end of 2008, I started TheCreativePenn.com.

Three years later, in September 2011, that blog enabled me to give up my full-time job because I now had a global plat-form for my books, courses, and speaking business, and I was able to help thousands of people every week from my desk at home. Wow! Life-changing stuff.

So I love blogging as the basis to an author platform. But remember, I'm not just an author, I'm also a professional speaker and entrepreneur. I sell products and recommend services beyond just books, so I have a small business that needs marketing, as well as my books. Your situation might be different.

My business developed out of blogging, and after starting on the journey, it may happen to you, too. Opportunities come from having an online platform.

Here's what blogging could do for you.

Attract an audience who know, like and trust you and who are interested in what you have to say.

People are more likely to find you on the Internet if you have content that is regularly updated, as Google, and people, love new stuff. Blog software allows you to update your site whenever you like, creating extra pages and posts for your website. These are indexed and over time, you can build up a great Internet presence so that people can find you easily when searching online.

Develop a voice and practice writing.

I have definitely become a better writer because of blogging for years. You have to shape your thoughts for an audience. You learn about structure and which ideas resonate. You learn to identify and articulate your own feelings and emotions more powerfully. It also gives you confidence that your writing can touch people because you get a response so much faster than with a book.

I don't think that I would be writing fiction without having blogged for years first. I spent 13 years trapped in a cubicle, my creative brain had atrophied, and I needed a way to oil the wheels again. If you're feeling that way, blogging can be a great kickstart to your writing.

Promote your book, business, or speaking career and develop an online sales channel.

Most of the top bloggers use content marketing as an engine to drive sales for all kinds of products – books, software, speaking, services, digital products, affiliate sales, consulting. So if you're considering setting up a small business, or if you already have one, effective blogging can expand your market tremendously.

Develop a reputation and connect with peers or like-minded people in your niche.

This is one of the most important benefits of the platform that so many underestimate. Being a professional blogger opens up a new world of networking. You can connect with other authors who blog, or literary agents, publishers and communities all over the world. It gives people something to base an opinion on, and if you control that perception, it can be a powerful start to any relationship.

Create a community with two-way interaction.

You can allow comments on your blog so that people can connect with you directly. You can also comment on other blogs. This allows a group interaction that cannot be achieved by a static website or email only.

When I have shared things on my blog that impact me personally as a writer, I love the subsequent conversation in the comments. It reminds me that I am not on this journey alone. One post on permission got nearly 200 comments, which added to and extended the conversation into the community. Social media and Facebook groups have replaced comments in some areas, but it's still a way to facilitate community.

Decide what you want to do with your life.

It might look like I designed TheCreativePenn.com as a business from day one, as if building the site was purposeful for selling my books. But when I started the blog, I would have sworn blind that I would never be a fiction writer. I thought I was going to be the British Tony Robbins, a self-help guru extraordinaire! As it turned out, the site does help people, but in a slightly less extroverted manner, and I ended up learning enough about myself over the years to make the leap to fiction. My blog helped me to decide what to do with my life. You might find that yours does the same for you.

Don't blog if you try it and hate it.

Or if your word count for your books is so high that books become your content marketing platform instead. There are plenty of other methods that you can use for marketing without content marketing.

You also have permission to start a blog and then give it up! I've given up four other blogs over the years. Experience is never wasted and if you're just not enthusiastic about it, then let it go.

Don't start a blog around one book, because there will be other books and you will change over time. Start something you can use long term. If in doubt, use your name as the URL.

* * *

So, you need at least a basic site with an email sign-up list, but you don't need to blog.

You get to choose. There are no rules.

4.10 Mistakes authors make with blogging

If you do go ahead and start a blog, it can be disheartening at the beginning because you won't have much traffic. Like your books, your blog audience will take time to build.

However, there are some common mistakes that I've seen many authors fall into that make things even harder.

(1) The site isn't built on a platform that encourages discovery

I'm not going to get uber-technical here, but your site needs to have efficient underlying code that enables search engine web-crawlers to find and index its content. You also need to be able to easily maintain your site yourself, so you can update it over time without handing the power over to a developer.

I recommend using self-hosted WordPress as the best software for your site, and you can use plugins to improve your site's effectiveness. For example, I use search engine optimization plugins like All In One SEO Pack which uses keywords to make your posts findable.

Check out my tutorial on how to build your own author site in 30 minutes at:
www.TheCreativePenn.com/authorwebsite

(2) Your design sucks

If you're using a free Blogger site with a standard theme, it will likely impact your brand and credibility. You need to give a professional impression with a site that looks like you care about your online presence if you want people to stick around. It doesn't have to cost you much for a great design.

I use Studiopress premium themes for WordPress, which are reasonably priced:

www.TheCreativePenn.com/studiopress

Design and usability also matter more since Google changed their algorithms to reward original, high-quality and high-value sites that have good usability and fantastic content. Your site also needs to be mobile optimized, which is covered by Studiopress with responsive design.

(3) Your headlines don't stand out

This is a biggie. Knowing how to write a book is not the same as understanding copywriting, which is writing to encourage action. The initial action you want from someone browsing for content is to read further than the headline.

There are lots of online tutorials about writing headlines. I recommend Copyblogger.com, where I learned about copywriting. The main thing is to put yourself in the mind of the reader. I see author blogs with headlines like 'How I parent my kids,' or 'My day at the modern art exhibition.' Turn this around to be something that someone else might want to read. For example, '10 ways to talk to your kids about money,' or '7 lessons learned about creativity from the modern art exhibition.'

Stop thinking about you, and think about the reader. This is good advice for marketing in general!

(4) You're not providing a benefit to your audience

The content of your blog is entirely up to you, but you do have to keep the reader in mind. What will they get out of your site? Once you know what you are aiming for, then deliver that every time. A blog is not a diary of your life, at least, if you're taking it seriously as a marketing tool. It's also not just a place to promote your book.

Provide useful information if you are a non-fiction author or small business owner wanting people to buy products. This is my model for The Creative Penn. As a fiction writer, you could focus on specific aspects of your research and topics your audience might find interesting.

Many fiction authors provide **entertainment**. Check out YA author John Green on YouTube at VlogBrothers as an example.

Your site should also enable an **emotional connection**. Sharing more personal, emotional aspects of your life can resonate with readers, and that connection persists over time. If in doubt, go deeper. This will foster a sense of **community**, and that will keep people coming back.

(5) Your content isn't original

People don't want to read the same stuff over and over again, so make sure that you are posting things that are original and in your voice. This is especially important for authors, as our distinctive voice is what makes people interested in reading our books.

Don't copy and paste whole articles from other sites, as you might get a Takedown notice from the creator.

You can, however, quote from or use parts of other people's

content, particularly if you want to build on it or comment on it. The Passive Voice blog is the best example of a site doing this, aggregating useful content but curating it and often commenting along with a link back to the original.

(6) Your content isn't focused enough

This is more relevant to non-fiction authors, but if you're trying to rank for a particular keyword or phrase then you need to focus your content around that topic. For example, at TheCreativePenn.com I blog about writing, publishing, book marketing and creative entrepreneurship. Although my life also includes aspects like travel, scuba diving, health, book reviews, chocolate, wine and other things, I don't include them as key parts of my site, so I rank highly for my target keywords.

(7) Your posts aren't shareable

If people like your content, they will want to share it online, but it needs to be easy to do. You can use a WordPress plugin like Social Warfare which will put share buttons on your post so people can Like on Facebook, share on LinkedIn and other sites easily. This will enable people who are on your site already to share.

You should also share your post on multiple sites so that people can find it. Whenever I publish a new blog post, I add it on my Facebook page, on Twitter, on G+, LinkedIn, and also StumbleUpon. If you have great images or video, you can also share on Pinterest, or whatever other sites you're active on. This will enable people on the social networks to share your posts without being on your site first.

Make sure that your social handles are clearly marked on every page. I surf a lot for useful content and just ignore any site where it is hard to find a Twitter handle to attribute the post.

(8) You're only hanging out on your own site

If you're not socializing online, how will anyone know your site exists? You need to get off your site in order to bring people back to it. A few ways of doing this include guest posting on other sites that are bigger than yours, networking on social media and commenting on other blogs, forums, or Facebook groups.

(9) You haven't given it enough time and effort

Some blogs seem to burst onto the scene, but often that's because the blog is not the writer's first attempt and they have learned a lot of lessons and made a lot of contacts along the way. They also guest post, pay for traffic, and get the word out more quickly. For most of us, growth in audience is mostly about time and effort, and that's also true of our book readership.

For the first nine months of The Creative Penn, I felt like I was howling into the wind and that no one would ever find me. After about a year, things started to happen, and it's been like a snowball, growing bigger over time. Years and thousands of posts later, my site is regularly listed as one of the top sites for writers and self-publishers online.

* * *

So if you want to use blogging effectively, set-up your site correctly, deliver value to your target market over time and make it easily shareable.

4.11 Guest blogging

It takes years to build up a devoted audience online and sometimes you don't have the time (or the inclination) to do this. But you can access other people's audiences by guest blogging, that is, writing an article or doing an interview for someone else's blog. This is particularly useful as marketing for non-fiction authors.

How do you decide which blogs to approach?

Think about your target market, then consider which blogs have that kind of person as their existing audience. This can be obvious or tangential. For example, you have a romance novel set in a New York yoga studio. You could approach blogs that specialize in New York city life, dating, yoga, as well as romance review blogs.

If you have a book about reducing Type II diabetes through Gluten Free food, you could approach healthcare and GF blogs as well as Mommy blogs concerned about childhood obesity and cooking blogs.

You can find these sites by Googling 'top blogs' in a niche, or use AllTop.com to search under specific areas. Once you find a couple, you'll find other similar ones through articles they refer to, or follow the blogger on Twitter and follow the people they follow.

How do you pitch them?

First of all, you need to follow the blog and get to know the tone and style of the blogger as well as the topics they cover. Check whether they even accept guest posts for a start, and what kind they want. Check their guidelines and be sure to follow them.

I get pitched every week by people wanting to blog about credit cards or online universities, neither of which are my niche, so I delete them without replying because it just shows a lack of interest in what my site is about. I also get pitched by a lot of authors who don't read the guidelines and write inappropriate articles. So make sure you follow the guidelines and also read a number of the blog posts so you can emulate the style of the site.

Remember that bloggers have usually spent a number of years and thousands of hours writing for and nurturing an audience. It is an extreme act of trust to allow you to speak to them, so the tone needs to be appropriate.

Pitch professionally, with respect for the blogger's time. Something like the following example, with name and detail changed to suit the particular situation of course.

* * *

Dear Mary,

I've been following your blog for a while now, and I loved your recent post about daily word counts and time management. I've got a book coming out in two months' time and wondered if I could pitch you an article about how to write a novel while working full-time and being a single parent.

Would that topic interest you? Or I could pitch you some other ideas if that doesn't suit.

You can see some of my other writing online here <insert site as appropriate>

Please do let me know and thank you for your time,

Joanna

* * *

It's easier if you have established a relationship of some kind first, for example, you have been conversing on Twitter or Facebook or at least retweeted their content or commented on their blog.

It's also easier if you have a blog of your own or have some examples of articles you have written to demonstrate that you can write this type of content, but that isn't always necessary.

Create your content promptly

Once you have been accepted for a guest post, make sure you know what date the blogger wants the content. Some blogs will ask you to log on and enter it yourself. Others will accept a Word document.

Make sure that you follow the guidelines, for example, the site may require a specific word count and also a photo and bio. They may require the post ten days in advance or even earlier so that they can have everything scheduled in time. With images, make sure you propose one of your own or royalty-free or Creative Commons licensed image and send the appropriate links.

Promote the post and be active in the comments

Once the article goes live, promote it to your audience on your blog or social networks. Subscribe to the comments on the post and actively participate in any conversation. Remember that comments can sometimes be posted months later, so subscribing means that you will always be able to pick them up later.

4.12 Image marketing

Think about how you scroll and surf through social media. In a sea of content, it's usually images that interest us the most. Studies show that posts with visuals get more engagement on social media. It's the same concept as book covers, and we all know that people *do* judge a book by its cover, right? So what are your options as a writer to use visuals in content marketing?

(1) Share ad hoc images on your social media timeline

When people tell me they don't have time for marketing, I usually point them to a smartphone and the use of pictures for shareable content. A picture creates a moment of connection, and someone will likely comment on it, favorite it or click to follow your profile because of it. These are not pictures of you and your book, just something you see or that inspires you. It will only take a few minutes to snap the picture, edit and share it.

Attraction marketing is based on being useful, interesting, inspirational or entertaining – and you can do that with just one picture a day. You might think your life is boring or mundane, but where you live might be fascinating to people on the other side of the world, or even in the next state. Try sharing pictures on Instagram, Facebook, Twitter or Pinterest and see who discovers you.

(2) Use images on your author website and especially on blog posts and articles

Many authors blog with no visuals to entice the reader, but your words are not enough in this era of short attention spans. Your article must also look enticing enough to read. Internet readers scan and images can give a good overview of what the article is about, so use them throughout your posts.

There are also plugins, like Social Warfare, that you can use on your website to ensure links are shared with suitable images.

(3) Make shareable images using quotes from your books

There are lines within your books that will be perfect for sharing. First, you have to find them, and if you have enough sales on the Kindle and people have highlighted passages, you can find them at kindle.amazon.com/your_highlights

If you have bought your own book, you can find it in your book list and then you'll see Popular Highlights listed on the page. You can, of course, go through the book with a highlighter and find quotes you like that way. You can also use quotes from other authors.

(4) Use Pinterest for story-boarding, research and inspiration

I love Pinterest, and I create a Board per fiction book project at Pinterest.com/jfpenn.

It helps me capture ideas and images during the process

of writing, as well as providing an extra dimension for my readers as I also share the pictures on my Facebook page. I include the Pinterest Board in my Author's Note at the back of my books. Register at Pinterest.com and download the Pinnable icon for your browser, then you can pin away while you're doing book research.

(5) Use infographics

These are perhaps best used for non-fiction books or for blog surveys or other useful information that begs to be shared. If you're someone who loves to play in PowerPoint/Keynote or Excel, you can prep the data there or use a free service like Canva.com which has templates. You can also use services like Infogr.am or Easel.ly or hire someone from Fiverr.com or PeoplePerHour.com to create one for you.

(6) Use SlideShare

Create PowerPoint or Keynote presentations that are heavy on the visual side and load them up to SlideShare.com. From there, they can be shared easily on any social media and embedded within your LinkedIn profile or other online platforms. You can find my non-fiction Slideshare at Slideshare.net/JoannaPenn

How to find pictures and make great images with the right dimensions

You can use your own photos or download Creative Commons licensed images from Flickr.com, so it doesn't have to cost you any money. Use the Advanced search option and then make sure you link back to the image owner. You can also get royalty-free images from Pixabay. com and other sites like BigStockPhoto.com. Just make sure the photos you use are 'royalty-free' and follow the license directions, so you are not infringing anyone else's copyright.

Each of the social media websites use images at different dimensions e.g. a Facebook header is different to a Facebook ad or a Twitter post. But don't worry, you can use Canva. com or PicMonkey.com to create images with the right dimensions. They also have templates, stock images, and various effects so that you can create professional-looking images easily and quickly. I use Canva most days to create images for various things. It's super easy to use and free unless you buy elements for your finished work. They even have templates for Kindle book covers.

4.13 How to sell books using social media

"Content is fire. Social media is gasoline."

Jay Baer, author of *Youtility:*
Why Smart Marketing is About Help not Hype

Social media is a mixed blessing for most people. On the one hand, it provides community and friends who we might never have met in real life, people who 'get us' even if they live on the other side of the world. It enables us to reach targeted readers and attract those who might enjoy what we write. On the other hand, it can be a huge time-suck with hours spent down pointless rabbit holes and has significant privacy issues.

You don't need social media to be successful as an author, but it can be used effectively if you set your boundaries.

Personally, I choose to use social media as part of my author business, to build community, talk to author friends, and advertise to potential readers. I also find it to be a brilliant form of marketing for introverts, because you can choose when you interact, and you can be at home alone in silence and yet still be 'out there' connecting with people. You can also schedule a lot of activities so that you can control your time. Apart from my blog and podcast, I would say that Twitter has played the most significant role in my online career, because of the relationships and opportunities that have arisen from connections there.

In many ways, social media is still about hand-selling to individuals, but this time on a global scale. It's about connection and relationships because behind every profile is an individual. The best way to use any of the sites is to be authentic and real. Don't broadcast spammy sales messages, just be yourself.

So, does social media sell books?

The adage goes, *"50% of marketing works. We just don't know which 50%."* It is indeed an inexact science, but here's how the marketing principle AIDA works for social media.

(1) Attention

Attention is hard to get in this speedy online world. Millions of books compete for it, as well as perhaps the more powerful media of TV, film, and gaming. Social networking is a way to attract attention for a moment in order to draw people into your funnel. Pieces of content are breadcrumbs leading to your door.

It could be a picture of the tequila your character drinks shared on Pinterest. It could be sharing a piece from National Geographic that your niche audience would find interesting. It could be a link to an article you've written about an art gallery launch that sparked your creative flow. Be interesting, entertaining or inspirational and be sure to use an enticing headline and image so that people want to click and share.

(2) Interest

Social networking is pointless on its own as a marketing mechanism (although of course it can be enjoyed for its own sake). The aim is to get people to notice you and be interested enough to follow you or click through to your website. Make sure that you have all your social networking links on every page or the sidebar of your site so that you are easy to connect with.

Social networks rise and fall. You don't own that real estate, you only borrow it for a while, so be sure to capture people's interest with a sign-up so you can develop this fledgling relationship further.

(3) Desire

Sometimes people will buy your book as soon as they hear about you but generally, it takes time for people to make a buying decision.

Once people have found you and are interested in what you're doing, they might follow your blog, maybe listen to an interview with you and continue to follow you on social networks. They may also receive your email newsletter. By producing other pieces of content, you will expand the impact you can have over time.

Social networking is about people knowing you, liking you and trusting you enough to let you have a slice of their time and attention. Authenticity over the long term is therefore important so that you can sustain this. Marketing, like writing, is a long-term activity. You might share snippets and pictures from your writing life while you're writing your book on social media and in this way, those who follow you will be ready to buy when you launch.

(4) Action

Once people know you, like you and trust you, they are far more likely to try your books or recommend you to others. There is no hard sell necessary. This method is about attracting people who might be interested in what you have to say. Once you have their attention, and you've built up a desire to see what you're doing, you can now ask them to take action and buy your book.

Use 80:20 as a guideline

One of the biggest mistakes of social networking is to make it all about you. Check some author's timelines and it is all focused on their book, but people will quickly switch off from this and unfollow.

The focus should be on being useful, inspiring or entertaining, with occasional updates that promote your own material or talk about personal things. This also facilitates social karma and results in enhanced word of mouth. Check my Twitter profile @thecreativepenn, and you'll find a mix of other people's articles with my own. I try to balance 80% sharing other people's content, replies and RTs with 20% links to my own articles or books.

Social means social

Social networking doesn't work if you don't enjoy it or if you are unrelentingly negative. Networks are collective energy expressed in one place. If you exude negativity or hype or spam, then that's what you will experience in return. It is about enjoying yourself, joining a conversation, learning from people, sharing something interesting and making connections. Yes, it's actually fun!

Some people think that online relationships are somehow shallow or unreal, but for introvert authors, the online social world is often far preferable to networking events or parties in person. Friendships formed on Twitter can spill into Skype conversations, meeting up in person and support networks, as well as mutual promotion. I met most of my real-life author friends on Twitter first.

Use social media to connect with influencers

One of the best ways to connect with people – other authors, bloggers, journalists, and publishers – is to meet them on social media.

Most people's email inboxes are hideously cluttered and full of emails that have no obvious connection to real people. But on the social networks, you can show up with a positive attitude, something useful to say and a smiling face, and people will be more likely to read what you have to say.

This is how I have made online friends all over the world, and these connections have led to speaking appearances, income and promotional opportunities, as well as to indirectly getting an agent. So, how do you connect with these influencers, without being a creepy stalker?

Find them on your favorite social network – or better still, on theirs

Most high-profile people are on multiple social networks now. Make sure that your profile is populated and relates to their area of interest and that your site looks good in case they click through. Use a headshot photo of you and not some default avatar, because that's an immediate newbie alert.

Promote them first and be useful

Retweet their content. Like and comment on their posts. Link to them from your blog. Book reviews also score serious brownie points. Do this consistently over time (without being scary), and they will likely follow you back. They may well check your profile or blog, so be sure that it gives a good impression. This is the beginning of them noticing you.

Develop the relationship

This takes time, so you will need to invest some effort, and this is the point at which people can discern whether you are really interested or just after a promotional opportunity. People are not stupid, so this is a long-term strategy that you would only follow if you consider someone to be a contact worth pursuing.

Pitch them **but only if it's appropriate**

Once they have noticed you in some way, you can ask to submit a guest post or ask for an interview, or whatever it is you had in mind. Follow the guest posting guidelines if that is your aim, but you must spend time getting to know them and their style first. Learn about their audience and be polite and courteous in any communications.

I don't want this to sound like a formula because it's not. It's essentially making friends online, and for me, it's been life-changing, but at heart, it's all about forming genuine relationships.

* * *

Of course, **social networking isn't a magic bullet to sell millions of books**. It's just one tool in the arsenal of marketing activities that some people enjoy. But from my personal experience, it can result in book sales, and it's a lot of fun!

4.14 Social networking tips

"If you get bored with social media, it's because you are trying to get more value than you create."

Fast Company

There are lots of social networks, but the popularity of each will inevitably rise and fall. Anyone remember Myspace? Regardless of the latest tool, there are principles that apply to all, and some basic mistakes that you can avoid. Here are some tips for social networking.

Be useful, interesting or entertaining

If you want to stand out in a crowded market online, you have to offer something to people. Remember the phrase "what's in it for me?" Everyone wants to know things that will help them, or interest them or make them laugh or entertain them. If you're not offering something that they want, then you won't get attention. If you don't have attention, it won't lead to interest in you or action in terms of buying your book. So focus on being one of these things as the main pillar of your social networking. For example, I tweet useful links to blog posts on writing, publishing and marketing @thecreativepenn on Twitter.

Use multimedia

Engage people with images and videos as well as text posts. Questions also get a lot of interaction. If you share funny things or emotional quotes, you'll get a lot of shares. People are on Facebook to have fun, to laugh, to connect, so enable that. Don't spam. Don't tweet your own stuff all the time. You will go nowhere fast. If you want your post to be shared across other people's networks, it needs to resonate. That means it should have a good headline and good visuals.

Use the principles of generosity and social karma

There is an understanding online that we are not competitors, that this isn't a zero-sum game, that the pie just keeps getting bigger. In fact, those of us in the same niche post on each other's blogs, share content other than our own and promote other people's products, even if they overlap with ours.

The blogging and social media world is all about being generous with links, information, and help. It makes the community a positive place to be, and we all benefit. It generates social karma, and you will receive back in the measure that you give. I don't mean this in any spiritual manner, just that "what goes around, comes around," as in any community. Don't be negative or offensive and don't rant unless that's your brand. Social media is a public forum, so be careful how you portray yourself.

Be personal

You also have to be a real person. Intersperse updates about your life, your writing, and your photos with your content. People connect with people, not info-streams. I also recommend using your face on your profiles. It's much more personal to connect with someone specific rather than an avatar or random picture. Using the same picture all over the Internet will help people to recognize you across the networks.

But don't be too personal. You need to set your boundaries and strike a balance. For example, I have bad days just like anyone else, but I disappear from social media on those days, preferring to keep a positive vibe in public, because I know it will pass.

Think long term

Social networking is essentially hand-selling to people around the world, but you need to connect over a longer period before you try to sell your book. Many authors dive into social networking just before their book launch and then try to sell immediately, or try desperately to grow their following at the last minute. But it doesn't work like that. You need to be consistent and put in the effort to create relationships over time.

This is a long game. Luckily, authors are used to long-term projects! If you don't tweet or update or post for months, people won't follow you. Simple as that.

Decide on your niche and stick with it

People follow people they are interested in. Make sure your bio includes the niche you're tweeting in, and your interests as keywords. If you stay on topic, you will get followers who are interested in you, they will share your content, and you'll get more followers in the niche. And so it expands. If you don't stay on topic, your followers will be a mixed bunch, and you won't appeal to them all anyway. Of course, you can intersperse your stream with more personal things, but in general, people are more likely to be active followers around a niche.

Think global with social media scheduling and book availability

Online social networking opens up the world to your books. That is truly exciting, but only if you take advantage of the opportunity. I'm based in England but 70% of my traffic comes from the US, 15% of my podcast audience is in China, and many other countries are represented in my Twitter stream and blog traffic stats.

The only way to reach people everywhere on social media is to use a scheduler for your tweets. I use BufferApp and MeetEdgar, but you can also use SocialOomph or Hootsuite. Scheduling in multiple time zones means that you can appear in streams at different times of day.

However, you should also remember that there is only a point in connecting internationally if your book is also available globally, which is much easier if you self-publish.

Don't buy followers. Grow organically or use the platform's official paid ads

Don't use any paid services for Likes or Follows or anything that promises amazing instant platform growth. They are likely to be spam followers or bots anyway. If you want to pay for reach and traffic, then use the advertising option that each platform offers. It can be a good investment if you have a strategy for reaching your target market.

Be strategic and decide on what you want to achieve

Set a time limit to avoid time-suck, for example, 30 minutes a day during which you will share content, reply to messages and network. It's easy to use social media for procrastination, so you need to be hardcore about your time. Scheduling is a great way to deal with this, as you don't need to be on the sites to still be seen.

You also need to consider what you find fun and sustainable because social media is most effective over the long term. You can't start today and expect to have an audience who will buy your book tomorrow. You need to find a network that is fun for you and that you can sustain over the long term. Make it a part of your life.

Remember, if you only have one hour a day for your author life, then write your book.

Writing should always come first. But if you are going to try a social network, or improve your presence, then pick one that you can commit to. Give it a few months of focus, have fun, and see how it goes.

4.15 Examples of how I use social media sites

There are a lot of books and courses on how to use each of the social media sites effectively. There are also new platforms every month, and my aim with this book is to provide principles that will last over time, rather than prescriptive how-to or technical information. So, in this chapter, I'll explain how I use some of the main social networking sites in an integrated marketing strategy in the hope that it might provide some ideas for you.

It's worth getting an account at the main platforms, even if you're not planning to use them all. You can always just point them back to your website.

Twitter

Twitter is my favorite social network. It's where I hang out @thecreativepenn, and you can always get hold of me reasonably fast by tweeting rather than emailing. I've built a circle of friends there and I also use Twitter for business. I use one profile because I am so active that it's hard to maintain more. I use BufferApp and MeetEdgar to schedule a mix of content, blog posts that I think my audience might find useful as well as links to my articles and books. I also post a lot of photos from my book research and personal life and reply to messages, as well as retweeting content from people I follow.

When I share other people's content, I will attribute it using their @ handle so that they see I am sharing their content, a good way to network with influencers. The majority of my podcast interviews have come from relationships that I have developed on Twitter.

I use the Twitter app on my iPhone and also Tweetdeck on the Mac to manage my stream. I use hashtags like #amwriting to post updates on my current work in progress. I've never bought followers or used ads to grow my profile on Twitter. I've just grown it over years of effort. I joined Twitter in early 2009 and have been tweeting 24/7 since then, although most of that is scheduled and I probably only spend 30 mins a day on it.

Having lots of followers is certainly not necessary, but I have found that it helps with online reputation and generating opportunities.

Connect with me on Twitter @thecreativepenn

Facebook

I have a personal profile for family and old friends and public pages for The Creative Penn, JFPenn, and the sweet romance pen-name. It's worth using a Page for your author profile because it enables you to use the Facebook advertising platform and keep some separation with your personal life. It's also a good idea to do it for your author name or brand rather than a book name, because you're likely to write more books and that individual book page will be hard to maintain over time. I made this mistake with my first book and had to start all over again once I decided to write more books.

I post similar content to what I put on Twitter, but usually only once a day, and I often post more images and photo albums. I interact in the comments, but I have an auto-reply on my Facebook messenger that directs people to email me. Although I use Facebook, I don't spend much time on it, because it's not my favorite network.

I use the Facebook app on my iPhone and also the Pages

app as my virtual assistants have access to the Pages, so we manage them centrally. I use paid advertising on Facebook as outlined in chapter 3.5.

I engage in some Facebook groups for professional organizations like the Alliance of Independent Authors, as well as some smaller groups of authors at different levels. These change all the time, but you'll find people recommending them across the platforms. I also run my own Facebook Groups for my premium course members.

To be honest, I'm not a natural Facebook user, as I don't like to chat a lot, and I almost left the platform a few years back, but now it is an important part of my business model. The ability to reach people through Pages and advertising is incredibly useful, and the Groups are great for staying in touch with what's going on in the indie world.

Connect with me on Facebook:

www.Facebook.com/TheCreativePenn

www.Facebook.com/JFPennAuthor

LinkedIn

If you have a business book of any kind or write non-fiction in general, then LinkedIn might be the place for you. It is the #1 professional and corporate network, and the average income of a LinkedIn user is much higher than users of the other networks. LinkedIn groups can be very active, and if you are the manager of a group, you can directly email people, so it can be a great place to build a community around a niche.

I have a profile on LinkedIn but I don't use it much. I post my blog articles there from TheCreativePenn.com so I have a presence, but not a particularly active one.

Connect with me on LinkedIn:

linkedin.com/in/joannapenn

Pinterest

Pinterest is based on sharing pictures and videos, emphasizing a visual stream organized into thematic Boards. It's highly addictive and fun. I use it for my fiction, creating a Board when I start a new novel and collecting images there as I research and write.

The title of the Board often reflects the working title, for example, I have a Board for Ragnarok, which became Day of the Vikings. I share the Board during my writing process, embedding it on the other social sites and tweeting about it. I also include it in the Author's Note at the back of my books so readers can see associated images.

Connect with me on Pinterest: pinterest.com/jfpenn

Instagram

I have one Instagram account for my fiction brand, and I post pictures from my research trips and things from my life. I like the simplicity of posting pictures with very little text. I certainly don't use it in any strategic marketing way, but more for providing a personal glimpse behind the scenes.

Connect with me on Instagram:

www.instagram.com/jfpennauthor

Goodreads

Goodreads is a social networking site for readers. It's also owned by Amazon, so the data likely gets incorporated into the book recommendation algorithms somehow.

Your books will get automatically added from Amazon a short time after publication, but once you have an author profile, you can also set them up yourself and control the images and the text, so add that to your launch checklist. It's definitely worth making sure your author and book data is correct on the site.

You do have to have separate profiles per pen-name, which is a bit of a pain if you're using multiple pen-names as I do, but it's worthwhile as many readers want to review on Goodreads as well as the other stores. You can add photos, videos and a blog RSS feed, so your articles are automatically posted.

I've been on Goodreads for years now and have used it to track my reading habits as well as rate and review books as a reader. As an author, I use it for print book giveaways every few weeks. Giveaways can raise your author profile and also enable new potential readers to add your books to their To Read list. There are Author Events available, Groups for sub-genres, and Author Q&A opportunities.

Many authors are wary of Goodreads because there have been reports of difficult relationships with some of the reader and reviewer community. I recommend that you use it as a reader first and only engage when you understand the rules of the community.

Don't go into the various genre groups and pitch your book, but rather join in with recommending other books that you like, and over time, relationships will develop.

* * *

There are many more social networks and new ones spring up all the time. The platforms change, but the approach remains the same.

Be authentic, connect as a person, don't be pushy about your book, think long term.

If you decide to get into a social network, then commit to a few months of dedicated effort to see if you can use it effectively and then incorporate it into your marketing strategy and daily life.

4.16 Should you create a podcast?

A podcast is audio that is streamed and distributed over the Internet. Podcasts can be talk shows, interviews, lectures, novels or indeed, anything else you fancy producing in audio format.

The main advantage of podcasts is that listeners can download the audio whenever they want, instead of radio, which is available at a specific time of day. People can discover audio at any time and if they connect with the host, they are likely to download backlist episodes which makes it evergreen content.

As a listener, you can subscribe to a show and then episodes will download automatically to your device. The most common podcast players are iTunes, Stitcher and Android players, but there are lots of different ways to listen. I personally love podcasts and listen to a number every week while walking, doing chores or going to the gym. I read books and skim blog posts and social media for information, but I deep dive on podcasting!

My podcasting journey

I started The Creative Penn podcast in March 2009. I had no audience and no author friends, but I was desperate to find a way to learn and connect with other creatives. For that first show, I put the phone on speaker and held a mp3 recorder next to it. Hardly a pro set-up, but at least I started! Podcasting was not as big as it is now and practically no one listened for the first year. But it didn't matter to me because I was learning and connecting, as I had set out to do. It was worthwhile for my author journey.

Fast forward a few years, and I was still podcasting every few weeks, releasing on an ad hoc schedule based on interviewing people I wanted to connect with. But I had started to focus on writing more books ,and podcasting took up a lot of time and effort as I did everything myself. I decided to give it up altogether, but then I took a look at the feedback and emails I received. Most of them related to the podcast and so many listeners told me it was valuable and useful to them.

So instead of giving the show up, I doubled down, moving to a weekly Monday show in mid-2015 and incorporating listener tweets and comments as well as doing a longer introduction about my writing journey. Many listeners say this is the most interesting part of the show!

I also started a Patreon page at Patreon.com/thecreative-penn, and listeners started to contribute financially. I also attracted a corporate sponsor to offset the costs of production. I now have a team of freelancers who help with the show, so I no longer produce the final audio, or format the YouTube video, or do the show notes and transcription edits. I continue to find the guests, prepare and conduct the interviews and write my introduction, but having a team makes a weekly show more sustainable.

That's my multi-year journey from a tiny new podcast to one of the longest-running shows for creatives. I also started a second show, Books and Travel, in 2019, which feeds my fiction and my wanderlust.

So why might you consider starting a podcast?

(1) Build a fanbase, a community and a platform

If you already listen to podcasts, you will understand why it's so powerful. If you let someone into your head for 30 minutes or more per week, you start to feel like you know them over time. You start to care what's happening in their life, and you're interested in what they're up to. There's also only limited time in the day, so most podcast listeners try a number of different shows and then remain true to their favorites, branching out now and then, but keeping a core number of shows that they listen to. Sounds pretty similar to our dedication to favorite authors over time, doesn't it!

Going back to the principle of know, like and trust, those fans who enjoy your podcast may also end up buying your books, products or services because you are fostering a long-term connection.

(2) Connect with peers and create relationships that go beyond social media

This mainly relates to interview-style podcasting. When I interview other writers and people in my niche, it facilitates a more authentic relationship between us. I often start off by meeting people on Twitter, then read their blog or books and then ask them on the podcast. I research them and send questions in advance, then when we get on the call, we have a quick hello and spend 45 minutes on Skype, often with video. After that amount of time, we have much more of a connection than we could have just by email or social media. In fact, many of the people I have interviewed on the podcast over the years I now consider to be friends.

It also builds up social karma, in that you are helping someone else by interviewing them. It can also create an immediate return, in that you are asked back onto their site or podcast, which will enable more marketing opportunities over time.

(3) Stand out in a crowded market

It might seem like there are a lot of podcasts, but there are actually relatively few because of the technical skills needed to get into the medium. If you consider how many millions of books there are, as well as millions more text-based blogs, podcasting can still be a way to stand out.

It may also be mature in some niches e.g. tech and entrepreneurship, but in many categories, it has yet to take hold. There is also room for varied voices, for example, an African-American female podcast on entrepreneurship will be quite different to a British male one. So don't think podcasting has peaked yet – you might just be the new voice in your market!

(4) The market for audio is growing

The consumption of audiobooks and podcasts has grown with the expansion of smartphones and faster Internet download speeds. This will only continue to grow as the Internet is expected to reach everyone in the world by 2025, and smart phones now cost less than $5 in India. The English-language audio market is expanding, and in fact, my podcast has listeners in over two hundred countries, which is pretty crazy!

Audiobooks and podcasts also reach a different audience to those who read text. They listen while driving, or doing physical jobs or chores, or at the gym or walking. They still consume story and information but in a different way. Why does it make a difference whether someone reads your work with their eyes, or listens to it? It still gets into their brain, and they can still connect with it, and with you. You won't reach this audience unless you're on audio.

(5) Incoming links and search engine optimization

When you interview someone, they will often link to that interview from their site as well as sharing it through their social networks. If your interviewees have a large network and a well-ranking site, this can increase your site's authority, and over the long term, all those incoming links improve your ranking and therefore, your ability to be discovered online.

(6) Learning and fun!

I love my podcast. It's fantastic to connect with people, and my main reason for interviewing is still to learn something new from people who know more than me about a topic. By putting it out there for free into the world, I hope other writers can learn along with me, plus the interviewee might get new fans, so it's a win-win for everyone.

My show has grown from zero listeners at the beginning to around 10,000 downloads per episode. It's still a marketing channel for me, but it's also an integral part of my life and the lives of my listeners. I don't intend to give it up at this point!

(7) Add another income stream

Let's be clear, most podcasts do not make any money. The same applies to most blogs, and in fact, most books don't even make enough money to cover the time spent creating them. But the financial aspect should be the last thing you consider when podcasting – or writing. The intrinsic value of podcasting makes it worthwhile for personal development and connections as well as confidence-building. My show certainly cost me a lot of time and energy over the first five years, but now the podcast is the backbone of my multi-six-figure business.

If you want to monetize your podcast, then you need to integrate it into a much more developed business model. I've outlined mine in *How to Make a Living with your Writing*.

The Creative Penn podcast now earns money directly through corporate sponsorship and Patreon support from listeners, but also indirectly through affiliate links and products that I talk about on the show, as well as being an important part of my non-fiction platform, so a lot of listeners buy my books and audiobooks. But this type of monetization only comes when you have built up an audience already and offered them value over time.

Check out The Creative Penn podcast

You can find the backlist episodes with all the show notes at TheCreativePenn.com/podcasts

The show is available on all the podcast apps and the interviews are all on YouTube.com/thecreativepenn

You can also support the show on Patreon and get an extra Q&A audio every month at Patreon.com/thecreativepenn

You can find Books and Travel on your favorite podcast app and the backlist at www.BooksAndTravel.page/listen

4.17 How to produce and market a podcast

If you're interested in podcasting, there are lots of resources that are dedicated to helping you design, produce and launch your show. In this chapter, I'll outline my process, including the technical tools I use. But remember, a bit like writing, there are many options, and you will find your best method once you give it a go.

How to decide on your podcast topic

Like blogs and non-fiction books, your podcast will be most successful if you focus on a niche. Check out the iTunes store under podcasts, and you will find them organized by category, and many of them include the topic in the show name. There are also personality-centric shows like mine which are based on what the host is interested in. These can be harder to categorize but also have more potential for the long term. If I had started my podcast around purely self-publishing, I would have been bored of it by now and started something new, but because it can be on anything 'creative', it remains fresh for me and the listeners.

Think about the topics of your books. What might lend itself to a specific niche podcast?

What type of show do you want to do? You could do a single-voice deep dive on a topic, like Dan Carlin's *Hardcore History*. His show involves huge amounts of research and is produced in series. Other options include a co-produced show with multiple hosts and occasional other guests like *Writing Excuses* or the *Self-Publishing Podcast*; or an individual host interviewing guests like my podcast or *The Tim Ferriss Show*.

Write down a list of people you might want to interview.

What do they have in common?

Podcasting fiction can also be incredibly powerful at building a fanbase.

Scott Sigler podcasts his fiction every week and has done for years, as well as providing free audiobooks for his fanbase. He has attracted an audience of raving fans that led him to a print publishing deal, the New York Times bestseller list and self-publishing his own series with special editions and a fan conference. All from an audio-based fiction platform. The rest of this chapter will be focused on the interview format, as that's what I do on my show, but if you want to podcast your novel, check out Scribl.com (previously Podiobooks) which has some great resources for authors, and lots of free audiobooks.

Here's how I produce *The Creative Penn* podcast. Although I now have virtual assistants to help me, I did it myself for the first six years of the show, and we still use the same process.

Step 1: Plan the show

I plan my interviews months in advance by contacting people with interesting books and proposing an interview. I usually create a relationship on Twitter first and read their books or blog for a while, or I might find an interesting interview with them on another site and contact them directly. I have a Google Spreadsheet with the planning schedule, shared with my virtual assistants, so everyone knows what is happening.

After arranging a time and date to call across multiple time zones, I email a week before the interview with a draft intro and questions based around a specific topic. I may veer off into other things when we talk, but the questions allow the guest time to prepare and they help me focus in case I get nervous, which I still do even after all these years!

Demonstrating professionalism through preparation is important, and I get antsy if people want to interview me and don't provide a similar level of detail.

Podcasting is an indirect form of marketing. It is more about awareness, and I make sure that my podcast is always focused on giving listeners actionable tips and information. However, I also realize that the guest wants to promote something at the same time, so I always ask the interviewee for their website address and to share more about their books or products. It has to provide value for everyone involved.

Step 2: Record the interview and create the raw audio

I use Skype video calls for all my interviews. It's free to call worldwide to other users and is cheap for calling phones. You need an add-on piece of software for recording, but it is reasonably priced.

For PC, use Pamela at www.pamela.biz

For Mac, use Ecamm Recorder at www.ecamm.com/mac/callrecorder

These create a video recording of the interview, which I then use to create a YouTube video version for my channel www.YouTube.com/thecreativepenn.

I use Screenflow for Mac to edit, although there are many

free and premium video editing options. Then I upload to YouTube.

If you don't want to do video, you can record audio only interviews on Skype, or some podcasters are now using zoom.us. You can also record audio straight into the software mentioned in editing below.

I use an AudioTechnica ATR2100 USB microphone. You can find the exact model at www.TheCreativePenn.com/mic

I have a MacBookPro, and I use the ear buds that come with my iPhone for sound. It's important to use a headset if you can, and get the other person to as well, as this will stop any echo in the room that you might hear on the recording otherwise.

Podcasts also have an intro and outro with some music and an introduction with the name of the podcast or the host saying hi.

Make sure you use royalty-free or Creative Commons licensed music, or your own if you're that creative. I used Soundsnap.com to find my intro music loop, but there are lots of options. To make your intro and outro, record audio directly, overlay the music and save these mini-files to add into each podcast at the beginning and end.

Step 3: Edit the audio

Even with the advent of high production quality podcasts like Serial, most listeners will forgive a certain amount of amateur production. After all, podcasts are free, and you don't need effects and fancy stuff unless you want to get that technical.

You can just record with a good microphone and then edit

the bad bits out. I leave umms, ahs, and little mistakes in as this humanizes people, but I remove what I don't want you to hear or if there are any technical problems, like loud background noise, or dogs barking.

For free editing software on PC or Mac, check out Audacity at audacityteam.org. I use Amadeus Pro on the Mac. Both of these are easy enough to use if you just want basic editing like cutting segments and splicing files.

I save the audio as a .aiff file out of Amadeus Pro and then use Auphonic.com to level the sound and add on the metadata, description, image, and keywords associated with the episode. It exports a completed .mp3 file.

Step 4: Distribute the podcast

You now have a finished audio file, but you still need to get it to people's devices. If you just load the audio to your site, people will have to download it manually and transfer it to their device, whereas if you use a podcast feed, it is automatically delivered to their mobile device.

I use Amazon S3 to host my finished files, so I upload the file there first. This gives listeners a dependable download speed even if there's a spike in listeners, as well as backing up the files in a secure environment. I also back up video and important files this way. It's incredibly cheap cloud hosting and the pricing scales based on traffic.

I use the free Blubrry.com Powerpress plugin for WordPress to create the play button and the download link on the blog post. Blubrry also have a hosting service if you don't want to use Amazon S3. Just paste in the hosted file URL into the plugin, and it does the rest. Blubrry also has its own feed service to iTunes, and you can easily follow the steps in the plugin or use their help. You get your initial iTunes feed by submitting to iTunes directly.

If you have more technical questions or want to take your podcast to a more professional level, then I recommend Cliff Ravenscraft at PodcastAnswerman.com

Step 5: Create show notes

For show notes, I get a transcription done through Speechpad.com. My virtual assistant edits the transcript and creates the show notes from this. I did it myself for years, but it's great to have help with this now as it's so time-consuming. There are services and assistants that specialize specifically in doing this for podcasters.

The transcript and show notes allow people to skim the highlights if they prefer to read information. It also ensures the post is indexed for SEO (search engine optimization).

I create an attractive graphic on Canva.com which helps make the post more shareable and use Social Warfare plugin on WordPress to enable easier sharing.

Once the podcast is live, I add it to the backlist episode page TheCreativePenn.com/podcasts as well as on Patreon, so it goes out to supporters. I schedule social media posts on Twitter and Facebook, as well as sharing to StumbleUpon, LinkedIn and Pinterest.

How to market your podcast

Discoverability is still an issue with audio because by it's very nature, it isn't searchable on the Internet. But you can take advantage of **Search Engine Optimization** by including detailed show notes or a transcript, as well as using an SEO plugin like Yoast, All-In-One SEO Pack or similar.

Your **podcast title** should also be similar to a blog post headline, outlining benefits to the listener first. For example: How to Write and Market a Non-Fiction Book with Joanna Penn, is a better headline than Episode 172: Joanna Penn on writing non-fiction. Listeners might never have heard of the interviewee, but they might care enough about the topic to listen in.

Make sure you have an **attractive image** for your overall podcast. I found that people connected more when I changed my podcast image to include my smiling face instead of just a logo. You can also use episode-specific images on your accompanying show notes page, which will encourage sharing. Some podcasters include **shareable images** for specific quotes as well.

You can also post podcast episodes on **SoundCloud,** which has a lot of sharing and embedding options built in.

Being a **guest on other related or even tangential shows** can help your profile among the podcast listener community. Target shows specifically and email the host outlining the topic you are an expert on and why you'd be a good fit for the show. Authors have an advantage here, as many podcasters like to interview experts with books. This can also work for fiction authors around the story themes, or pitching writing and creativity focused shows.

There are **podcast directories** and various lists that you can submit to, as well as topic-specific 'best podcast' lists. These change over time, so Google for the latest ones. Getting **reviews** on your podcast will also help over time, as will building a specific **podcast email list**.

When you first launch your show, it's recommended to have a number of episodes ready for people to listen to immediately. It's common practice for new podcasters to launch with **10-15 pre-recorded episodes**, because it takes time to become a habit for a new listener and you want them to be able to binge.

For a discussion on **tactics and technology for podcasting**, as well as tips on how to be a good guest on a show, check out this interview with Jerod Morris from *The Showrunner* podcast at www.TheCreativePenn.com/jerod

Is podcasting worth it?

Podcasting takes a LOT of time, approximately four hours of prep and production for every one hour of finished audio, and there are very few podcasters making any money directly from their shows. So, it is *not* something you do primarily for income as there are far easier ways to make money.

But podcasting is great if you start doing it because you want to learn and help others, connect with your audience and build a long-term platform using your voice. If you're going to podcast, then commit for at least six months. If you make it that far, you'll be hooked. It's definitely been worth it for me.

For more details on everything you need to know about podcasting, check out *Audio for Authors: Audiobooks, Podcasting, and Voice Technologies.*

4.18 Video marketing

Many authors seem to think that the only way to use video as an author is to have a book trailer available. But creating one video, of any kind, is the least effective way to utilize this powerful medium. There are lots of options for using video marketing, and you can even just use your smartphone these days. You don't need loads of expensive equipment.

Why is video great for marketing?

YouTube is owned by Google and is either the #1 or #2 search engine on any given day. YouTube has over a billion users, and over 500 million hours of video are watched on it every day. In fact, one study reports that one-third of online activity is spent watching video, increasing as social media focuses on video too.

If you have a lot of videos on a particular topic, your channel will become a place that people subscribe and return to. People are also increasingly used to consuming long-form video on YouTube as more TV shows are available for streaming.

Video is great for instant connection.

If people know you, like you and trust you, they are more likely to buy your book. When people see your face and your smile when they hear your voice, they will make a decision as to whether they like you. The greatest proportion of human communication is non-verbal, which can't be communicated in plain text.

Voice recognition is improving.

Google is developing voice recognition and automatic captioning so that videos will be more easily searchable through text-based algorithms. This means that your ranking for a particular topic could be fantastic if your videos are around niche keywords.

As AI universal translation services improve, viewers may also be able to consume your work in other languages.

Video can be the basis of your platform if it suits your style and personality.

Video can drive traffic to your main author site if you add show notes under the video or a website link in the video. This increases your traffic and hopefully your subscriber list and sales.

It helps you stand out because so few authors do video. It is especially valuable if you want to speak or if you have a business that goes beyond the book.

There are many options for video content. Here are just a few:

Vlogs or talking head opinion pieces

Many of the big YouTubers do this, whether it's in their bedroom or out on location. It's about sharing your thoughts on life, or on themes that resonate with your book. It's usually done every day as a slice of life, although it's often heavily edited. YouTubers jump cut between scenes or intersperse with other video clips or music. The most important thing is to create videos that appeal to your target market and give them an insight into your life.

A great author example of an author vlogger is John Green, New York Times bestselling author of *The Fault in Our Stars* and other books for young adults. His YouTube channel VlogBrothers, created with his brother Hank, has nearly three million subscribers. John and Hank connect with their audience by creating the type of videos that their demographic enjoy – fast-talking, attention-grabbing, crazy-loud talking, almost-daily vlogging covering everything from nerd jokes to explanations of political events. They educate as well as entertain, and their Nerdfighter fans love them for it.

You can find one of my opinion videos, filmed outside the London Library on a winter morning, at:

www.TheCreativePenn.com/fictionliveson

Interviews

The majority of my YouTube videos are Skype interviews for my podcast, but they can also be on location. I post the whole video as one long interview, whereas most likely it would be better to do multiple clips with more specific segments. But as video is a secondary channel for me, I choose to leave it unedited. You can find an interview with Steven Pressfield, author of *The War of Art*, *Turning Pro* and many more great books for authors at:

www.TheCreativePenn.com/pressfield

Product review videos

There are lots of vloggers who focus on reviewing products like makeup through tutorials and demonstrations. For authors, review videos are posted by BookTubers who you can pitch with your book if appropriate as it must be a beautiful physical product for them to consider reviewing it.

How To instructional and teaching videos

When our sink blocked recently, we went straight on YouTube and found a video to help us fix it. This type of practical video is super useful and ranges from pronunciation tips to knitting, to using Dragon for dictating your book and many more examples that would suit non-fiction authors in particular. You can film the activity or use screen capture software like ScreenFlow for Mac or Camtasia for PC, which is great if your book is about software or online tools.

Another variation is the webinar or presentation-style teaching format. You can find a recording of a webinar I did on How to Write Fiction as a Non-Fiction Author at:

www.TheCreativePenn.com/writefictionvideo

Time-lapse video

If you use your smart phone for video, there are all kinds of cool apps you can use. I used the TimeLapse app to create a video about book-binding available at:

www.TheCreativePenn.com/bookbinding

It doesn't market my books in particular, but it's more about that first glimmer of attention with content marketing. This type of video might lead to someone considering you interesting enough to start following.

Facebook Live videos

You can now broadcast directly from your Facebook Page, and many authors are sharing 'on location' videos or behind the scenes at their writing desks or on research trips. They're also doing live Q&A sessions. I've done a few of these, and you can download the video later and post it on YouTube, repurposing the content. You can find one of my recorded Facebook live sessions at:

www.TheCreativePenn.com/facebooklive

If you want to try one, just go into Facebook, click Publish and then choose Live Video.

You can also post your other videos on Facebook and other social media. Over half of video content is viewed on mobile, so it is well worth utilizing these mobile-first video platforms. I found that engagement on my Facebook Live videos was high, but to be honest, I am not a fan of doing live video, so consider what works for you.

Book trailers

These can range from movie-style trailers that are out of the budget of most indies, to reading from your book or a DIY version compiled yourself from royalty-free music and video clips.

My main issue with book trailers is that some authors think that one video will make all the difference to their sales, but it rarely does. The most successful people in video marketing online are putting videos out regularly, so fans develop a viewing habit over time.

Book trailers can be great if they're done well or used as part of a campaign, but the return on investment is hard to track, and there are better ways to spend a marketing budget.

For the really professional side of things, check out Tim Ferriss's blog post on how to create a viral book trailer or get a million views for almost anything at:

www.TheCreativePenn.com/timbooktrailer

Tim's book trailer for *The Four Hour Chef* is indeed awesome, but certainly beyond the budget of 99.99% of us.

I've made book trailers using royalty-free stock footage, photos and music and I've also hired professionals. Here are some of my examples:

- Self-made trailer for *Desecration*:
  www.TheCreativePenn.com/desecrationtrailer1

- Professional trailer for *Desecration*:
  www.TheCreativePenn.com/desecrationtrailer2

- Self-made trailer for *The Successful Author Mindset*:
  www.TheCreativePenn.com/mindsettrailer

Whatever type of video you make, remember that the usual copywriting rules apply to titles, so make sure that your videos have a compelling headline and you include a description and appropriate keywords and links in the description and tags so your work can be found.

For more tips on video production and YouTube marketing, check out this interview with author Michael La Ronn:

www.TheCreativePenn.com/michael

4.19 Marketing audiobooks

Audiobooks are the fastest-growing content medium for publishers, and the international spread of smartphones and faster Internet means they will only continue to grow.

You can license your audio rights, or use a site like ACX. com to find partners to work with on production, narration and distribution (currently only available to a small number of countries). You can also narrate, produce and distribute your work yourself, but you will need to up-skill for this to be at a professional level. Once you have the audio, you can distribute it to Audible, Amazon and iTunes, as well as many other retail platforms. But then, of course, you need to market those audiobooks because unfortunately, the likelihood of audiobook listeners stumbling across your book on Audible is pretty small. Here are some ideas.

Update your website with links to Audible and iTunes

Make sure that each of your website book pages include links to your audiobooks, and create a dedicated audio-book page that includes excerpts and links to buy on the various stores. Here's my own fiction page as an example: www.jfpenn.com/audio

Soundcloud.com has the option for including the cover as part of the Embed code, which makes the page look more attractive, and you can add your audiobook sample so people can try before they buy.

It's easy to include sidebar advertising on a blog, and promoting your own books is a great way to use that real estate.

Remember to mention that you have audiobooks whenever you do an interview or talk about your books. For example, I do a lot of podcast interviews these days, and I always say "My books are available in ebook, print and audiobook formats at the main online stores," so people know they can get the books in audio format.

Use audiobook promo code giveaways

As with ebooks and print, reviews are critical to provide social proof and convince people to buy your audiobook. If you already have your book in other formats on Amazon, it will be linked to the other format reviews, but for Audible and iTunes, you need separate reviews.

ACX will provide 25 review codes after your audiobook is released and you can email them for more. You can get promo codes on iTunes for all your products as well. You can run giveaways for those codes on your email list or podcast, run a competition on social media, or provide them to your Street Team.

There are also sites that specifically review audiobooks, like audiobookboom.com or audavoxx.com. Search for those by genre and only pitch those who like books similar to yours. If you are an audiobook listener, you can always email me about getting a free review copy of one of my books.

Create shareable links to your audiobooks and schedule on social media

I use MeetEdgar.com to schedule my social media. I have several tweets with links to my audiobooks that go out automatically every few weeks. I use a composite image that I created on Canva.com with my audiobook covers. You can also use these images in paid ads on Facebook and in your email newsletter. I sometimes have an audiobook section in my reader updates.

Promote your audiobooks on podcasts

If you have your own podcast, you can use it to promote your audiobooks. This sounds obvious, but I only started advertising my books on my own show in the last year! You can also pitch other podcasts for an interview spot – just make sure you target specific shows that focus on your niche.

Work with your narrator to create an excerpt with atmospheric (royalty-free) music if possible. You can use that on your own podcast or pitch related podcasts to include your trailer. There may be paid opportunities for promotion on some shows, but only pitch if your book is appropriate for their audience.

You can also release audiobooks for free with Scribl.com, formerly Podiobooks, which has subscription feeds like a podcast but is for full-length audiobooks. As with anything free, it works best when you have a series of other books available to buy.

If your fiction books are short, create audiobook boxsets

I've found that fiction audiobook boxsets are much easier to advertise and sell than individual novels, especially if the audiobooks are under eight hours on Audible. My London crime thriller trilogy boxset sells many times more copies than the individual books. This is because the majority of listeners on Audible have a subscription and they want value for that monthly payment. The price of books on Audible is determined by a number of factors, one being length, so a shorter novel is not as good value as a much longer one. I haven't found this bias with non-fiction audio.

Use spike marketing like BookBub to promote the ebook

Your audiobook is connected to the ebook on Amazon, and if someone owns the ebook, they can buy the Audible version for a cheaper deal. So audiobook listeners wait for BookBub deals, get the ebook for free or cheap and then buy the lower-priced audio. It's a clever listener hack and one you can take advantage of. Schedule email list promotions like BookBub or BargainBooksy and you will likely also see a spike in audiobook sales.

Bake in marketing by using a narrator with a following

This is really only an option for authors with the budget for higher narrator investment, or authors who do audiobook rights deals. There are listeners who love specific narrator voices and will follow that narrator across projects, so if you use them as a voice talent, you may get crossover sales in the same genre.

* * *

These are some initial ideas for audiobook-specific marketing, but it's still a new arena. As the market expands, it's likely that more marketing options will arise as they did with ebooks over time. The next few years will be an exciting time for audiobooks!

For more details on everything you need to know about audiobooks, check out *Audio for Authors: Audiobooks, Podcasting, and Voice Technologies.*

4.20 Marketing print books

You should always think about marketing the *book*, rather than the specific *format*, but since most indie authors make 80% or more of their income from ebooks, most marketing activities are more geared in that direction. If you have print available, you will sell some copies just by it being an option for readers, and I've found that non-fiction does particularly well with print.

If you need more detail on publishing print, read my free ebook, *Successful Self-Publishing*, but it is important to note that if you want to do many of the things on this list, it's best to publish with IngramSpark, or another printer, as well as KDP Print. In this way, your book will be available in the catalogs that booksellers and libraries order from, and they will be able to get a discount, which is critical for print book sales through this channel. You can also choose to accept returns, although this is risky because you can end up losing money.

Here are some marketing activities that suit print in particular.

Advanced Reader Copies (ARCs) and review sites

Many book reviewers love print books, and although you can send a digital file, it's much easier to forget a book in the Kindle queue than it is a beautiful print book on your bedside table. Traditional publishers send out print copies to specifically targeted reviewers months in advance, sometimes with an embargo on reviews until launch, which generates buzz. You can use NetGalley.com to make your ARCs available to reviewers and offer an ebook version at the same time.

If you want to model traditional publishing, you will need to plan in advance and hold back your book from publication, even if it is ready (something many indie authors struggle with!). Use IngramSpark to set up your print book and send it to reviewers, setting an On Sale date in the future. Pitch reviewers with a professional package with all the information they need. You could also submit it for reviews at Publishers Weekly and other sites that need several months lead-time on reviews.

Literary festivals, book signings, and library events

There are more and more literary festivals springing up now, even in small towns. These usually involve panel discussions around theme or genre, interviews with authors, readings and book signings. I'm a regular at CrimeFest in Bristol, England and ThrillerFest in New York. My books sit alongside traditionally published books on the bookstall, and I sit on panels with authors who publish in all kinds of ways.

Some festivals still have issues about indies, but if you attend for a few years and make relationships over time or even volunteer, you can usually get on the panels and have your books in the store. Because there are so many authors, many more famous than you, it's unlikely that you will sell many books this way, but it can be a great way to expand your author network and meet bloggers and reviewers.

Book signings are often featured as part of these festivals, but they are usually only worthwhile if your target market attends. Otherwise, you may find yourself stuck behind a table with a pile of your books and no one talking to you. These signings are appropriate for big-name traditionally published authors but are not great for book marketing otherwise.

Events that are not specifically book-focused can be a great way to sell print books, for example, Christmas markets or summer craft fairs, as well as themed events around places or historical occasions. Basically, anywhere you can get a stall and sell your books.

Libraries often run author events, and they are always looking for people to speak. You won't get paid, but you might sell a few books and make some connections for next time.

Professional speaking events

Many non-fiction authors are also speakers and sell their books at the back of the room, and some may even include the price of books for the audience in their speaking fee. If you're running your own events, you can also sell your books directly to attendees. I usually just take cash or offer to PayPal invoice people later, but if you're doing these regularly, apps like Square enable card processing easily and cheaply. If you're speaking at a bigger event, you can arrange to include a book or a postcard in the attendee swag bags. If you're interested in speaking, check out my book, *Public Speaking for Authors, Creatives and Other Introverts*.

Direct mail and advertising to libraries and bookstores

In the same way that you can use Facebook advertising or BookBub to reach readers, you can also use specific advertising methods to reach booksellers and libraries. If you're serious about selling a lot of print books, you might consider joining an independent publishers organization. They have directories of booksellers and distributors, libraries and services that will help you sell direct and options to include your books in catalogues. For example, The American Booksellers Association offers opportunities to contact booksellers directly, and you can place ads in bookseller-facing publications like Publishers Weekly.

Relationships with bookstores

If you want to get your book into a physical bookstore, think about life from the bookseller's perspective before approaching them. They have to handle a lot of merchandize that makes a small profit, and they need to manage their overheads. Imagine if every book in the bookstore was sold by a different author and billed separately. The bookseller would spend all their time dealing with authors and paperwork rather than customers. This is why booksellers would rather buy multiple books from one distributor than lots of individual books from individual sellers. The distributor also offers a quality filter and has built-in marketing, as well as very often paying for specific placement or merchandising in the store.

The bookseller will require a discount on the print book in order to make any profit at all, so you will need to make your book available through IngramSpark and match the discount offered by other publishers.

Indie authors can get their books into bookstores in a number of ways, but the most important is through personal relationships. If you regularly buy books at your local bookstore and they know you, they are more likely to be open to stocking your book on their shelves. Perhaps you could even have a launch event there and bring more customers into the shop. You can also develop relationships with buyers for bookstore chains, as Carol Cooper did for her book, *Hampstead Fever*, which featured in UK national chain WHSmiths, along with airport and train station bookstores.

If you want to get into bookstores and libraries, the Alliance of Independent Authors has a great guide at www.TheCreativePenn.com/bookstores

Children's books in schools

Books for young children work well in print because they are often image-heavy, but this also makes them expensive as print-on-demand. Many children's authors do limited print runs and then sell direct into schools through school visits and by developing relationships with librarians. Most schools are happy to have authors come in and run a lesson or do an assembly. If you send the children home with information, you can sell books to parents as well as teachers.

If you develop on-going relationships, the school might buy books for the library, or you could sell them at school events. This takes a lot of work for a small amount of profit, so some children's authors focus instead on online print sales by targeting bloggers who review children's books like Mommy blogs or Boomer blogs for grandparents.

Special and bulk sales

Special sales and bulk sales are great ways to sell more print books. You just have to think differently. For example, if you have a book on pet care, consider pitching it to a pet store chain as something that could be co-branded and sold in their stores. If you regularly speak for a large organization and have a book on time management, consider offering to co-brand a special version of your book with their logo and offer it at a steep discount to be given to all employees in the holiday season.

Honoree Corder, author of *The Successful Single Mom* and other books, offers custom print runs for her books so that divorce attorneys can offer it to their clients as a gift and include their business details on the back. The book remains the same, but the back cover becomes an ad for the attorney, so they are more than happy to pay for printing costs plus royalty for the author. This model is more suited to non-fiction, but it's definitely worth thinking about. You can listen to an interview with Honoree at www.TheCreativePenn.com/honoree

Book clubs, writer's groups, or special interest groups

There are online book clubs like Goodreads, but there are also book clubs all over the world who meet in person to discuss books every week. Your book can be one of those.

Start by creating a list of questions that book club members could discuss about your book around theme, characters, or topics depending on the genre. Then search for directories of book clubs on Google, whether you want to look locally, nationally, or further afield.

If you offer discounts on your books, you might be able to organize bulk buying for the group. You could also offer to chat with the book club, either in person or via Skype, which I've done before with groups in Australia, the USA and Singapore. Borders are no problem with today's technology!

There are also writers' groups, as well as special interest groups who might want to read your books. Think about your potential market and then go deep into researching where they might hang out.

Crowdfunding beautiful print

Crowdfunding is a way to raise money for your creative project, but it can also be an effective marketing strategy. I don't suggest you use it for your first book or just a paperback version, but if you use it for a special project, it can draw people in and enable them to get involved.

Orna Ross, Irish literary fiction novelist, poet and founder of the Alliance of Independent Authors, did a crowdfunding project for her special edition of *Secret Rose*. It combined WB Yeats' novel *The Secret Rose* with Orna's own *Her Secret Rose* into one beautifully designed hardback with a gold embossed cover. The high print costs were covered by crowdfunding. Readers effectively preordered the limited edition, and then Orna sold more copies at premium pricing at live events for Yeats's anniversary celebrations.

Crowdfunding isn't a scalable or repeatable model, but it can be suitable for special projects that require higher upfront printing costs where the author has an audience and community ready to support them.

* * *

These are just some ideas for focusing on print sales in particular, and it's an area I'm personally exploring in more detail.

In early 2017, I set up Curl Up Press as a publishing imprint for The Creative Penn Limited and joined the Independent Publishers Guild in the UK as a way to try and start selling more print books. It's a small but growing segment of my own publishing business, but because so many of the marketing methods aren't scalable and take so much time, I tend to focus on online marketing.

The Bookseller reported that print sales online overtook print sales in bookstores in 2014, so you can still sell print books by focusing on scalable digital marketing. You get to choose what you want to do for your books.

4.21 Merchandizing

Merchandize can be defined as physical things that relate to your books, used for marketing or income purposes. It can range from the bookmarks, postcards and pens you see in swag bags at author events, to mugs or images with quotes on, all the way to action figures associated with Harry Potter or the rune-inscribed One Ring you can purchase to go with your Tolkien boxset.

Melissa Addey, author of *Merchandising for Authors*, explains that merchandize should increase your readership and visibility, add to your credibility and build your author brand, and potentially bring in income.

As human beings, we have an innate and entirely natural drive to belong to groups, and merchandize can be tribal. Providing merchandize for fans of your work offers them a way to feel a part of the tribe of readers you are attracting with your stories and books. Musicians have known this for decades. You must have at least one rock'n'roll t-shirt in your wardrobe! In the same way, authors can provide their fans with a way to connect more deeply with the books and characters they love.

Examples of author merchandize

You might automatically think of bookmarks, coffee mugs and t-shirts, and those are certainly popular choices for authors. But the range of items creatives can sell is limited only by our imagination. Here are just some of the things authors are merchandizing on their sites: autographed book plates, pillows, hoodies, tote bags, bath mats, notebooks, covers and skins for laptops and cell phones, and even charm bracelets hung with little books. The list could go on and on. If you use it in your home, you can probably find a way to merchandize it.

Authors use quotes and images from their characters, slogans, and business signs that their characters work for or own. For example, mystery writer James Lee Burke has a line of merchandize including baseball hats and t-shirts branded with the logo and slogan from his character Dave Robicheaux's Louisiana bait shop. Romance author J.A.Huss has merchandize for all her books, including mugs, t-shirts, pillows, prints, and much more. Check out her store for ideas at www.society6.com/jahuss

How to make merchandize

You don't need to spend lots of money because there are numerous services online that will allow you to add your design to a whole range of print-on-demand products. The customer orders their coffee mug or other piece of mer-chandize, a single item is printed with your design, and it is shipped directly to them. So, you don't need to order two thousand mugs up front, store them in your garage, and then mail them out, one at a time, to your customers. It's just like print-on-demand for books!

You receive a pre-arranged percentage of the purchase price, minus the cost of the product and the percentage that goes to the vendor site. Terms vary, depending on the vendor, so make sure to investigate before you sign up.

Popular sites for this type of merchandize are Society6, CafePress, Teespring for t-shirts, Spoonflower, Redbubble, or Zazzle.

Once you've decided on the product you want to create, hire a graphic designer to do a custom design for you. Your cover designer may be able to help, and might even have some ideas that would tie in well with your cover branding. You could also use a site like 99Designs. Make sure you know what the contract terms are when you purchase art to use in your design. If you (or your designer) use an image from an image bank for your design, make sure you understand the licensing conditions under which you are allowed to use that image.

Once the design is on the product, order one yourself to check the quality. Then you can promote it to readers, take some to events and add the links to your website.

Watch out for contract terms

Even if you're not interested in making merchandize yourself, be sure to have a clause in any contracts around your work that address the issue. If a publisher sells merchandize based on your intellectual property, it's important to be compensated fairly.

As a warning, Carrie Fisher revealed before her death that when she was a young actress, she signed away the rights to her own image before the Star Wars movies were released. Don't do that! One of your characters might just be the next Princess Leia. If you ever get that film deal, make sure that the contract includes a clause for merchandize because that can be a significant income stream.

4.22 Traditional media and PR

Many authors think marketing is all about appearing in national papers and magazines as well as on TV and radio shows. That's definitely one form of marketing, but as you've seen from the rest of this book so far, it's not the only one.

What is PR anyway?

Public relations encompasses communication between an author and the wider world. The term usually refers to appearances in print newspapers, magazines, TV and radio interviews and is facilitated by a publicist with contacts in the industry and in-depth knowledge of what might fit where.

However, having a publicist doesn't guarantee that you will make it onto national TV or into the newspapers. And even if you do make it into traditional media channels, that doesn't guarantee book sales.

PR is more about brand awareness and social proof than actual sales because it's a non-targeted, scattergun approach rather than focusing on a narrow target market as you can do online. There's also a disconnect between where people are when they consume that media and the jump to buying a book. Clickable links that go directly to a book retailer are much more effective for direct sales than a feature in a print magazine or an interview on TV or radio.

Of course, it's great to have both!

I made it onto national TV and radio and into national newspapers back in 2008 with my first book, but I only sold a few books in the same period. There was no sales spike at all. I was hugely disappointed, as I had spent a lot of time, energy and effort trying to get coverage in the press. I'd done everything I was supposed to do, and yet there was practically no result. I was in the national press and on TV again at the beginning of 2014, and once again, there was no sales spike.

So why doesn't traditional media (generally) work for selling a lot of self-published books?

It's not targeted enough.

Online marketing pinpoint a specific audience because of how fragmented it is, but traditional media broadcasts a message to a wide base of people, and only a tiny percentage will be interested in your book. Nowadays, media is fragmented into niches, and you are more likely to sell books if you market to your target audience rather than everyone.

It's too far from the point of sale.

When people are consuming traditional media like TV, radio, newspapers or magazines, there isn't a link for them to click to buy your book now, whereas with an online article, advert, email, blog post or social share, you can embed a link. People don't have to search for your book online, they just have to click if they are interested in buying.

Your book needs to be readily available in bookstores when people hear about you on traditional media. Debut authors and big brand names get a lot of press when their new books are released, as their books are placed on front tables in bookstores and supermarkets. But if your books aren't out front or even stocked, most people will forget they heard of you and buy something else.

There's no specific call to action.

The media is not interested in promoting your book, they are only interested in the story it fits into. So they won't give a specific call to action, for example, click here to sample or buy this book now, or even click here to try author X's new book. Most media will not even mention your website or your book buy links, because that's not their job.

So is traditional media worth it?

In saying all this, don't turn down media opportunities, because they are worth pursuing for brand recognition, as well as social proof. People are impressed by media exposure, even if it doesn't have any sales impact, and you never know what may come from it over time.

I include a picture of all the media I have appeared in on my author sites. It acts as social proof and opens up further opportunities. However, personally, I don't spend any time seeking out media placement. I'd rather spend my marketing time online, as it is more scalable.

Should you hire a publicist?

Authors are often introverts, and one of the worst possible things for us is cold-calling. I don't take phone calls in general, and I have to psych myself up for any that I *have* to make. Like most authors, I prefer writing.

A publicist is a professional marketer with experience in traditional media and relationships with particular outlets. They may specialize in book promotion in a particular genre, or be more of an all-round brand promoter. Importantly for an author, they will likely enjoy meeting people and making pitch phone calls and won't be upset when they get rejected by journalists or TV executives. The best publicists are persistent and follow up multiple times.

A book publicist is NOT someone who creates a press release and puts it online or sends it to thousands of journalists. This is spam. If you're offered this service, please run a mile, because your press release will just sink to the bottom of the virtual pile. I get way too many emails from authors who have bought this type of marketing service and then been terribly disappointed, so please be careful.

A publicist can pitch and follow up for you, but they can only work with what you provide, so you'll still need to think about the hooks that your book can be tied into. They will give you a weekly run-down of what they have done on your behalf, but paying a publicist won't guarantee you national coverage. It will get the publicist working on your behalf, but unless you have something newsworthy, it will be very difficult for them to make a significant impact. So what you get in return for your money will depend on how newsworthy you and your book are, what is currently trending and how your book hooks into it, the experience and contacts your publicist has, and how much they hustle on your behalf.

How can you find a good publicist?

Personal recommendations are the best way, so ask other authors online or through forums or writers' groups. You can also search online in your specific area if local expertise is important. Make sure that you check the publicist's credentials and their experience. Do they have testimonials from happy book clients? Can you contact those authors directly to find out what really happened?

You can also find publicists and other book marketing experts at the Reedsy Marketplace:

www.TheCreativePenn.com/reedsy

If you do engage a publicist, then you can help make the process successful.

Clearly specify your goals for the campaign and make sure that you understand what the publicist is offering and how much they are charging.

Identify your target market and where they might be found in terms of publications, online sites and more, and talk about it with your publicist. Go through your book and your life, **find all the story hooks you can think of** and provide a list.

Make sure you are media-ready, that your website and author photos are professional, and you can go on TV or radio at short notice.

Remember that you hire a publicist for a specific period (unless you have unlimited cash), so they are more about a spike in sales. You will still need the on-going marketing efforts that this book outlines if you want consistent sales over your career.

4.23 How to get media attention with a newsworthy story

No one cares that you have written a book.

Sorry, that might be hard to hear, but it's not news to say that there is yet another book in the world by yet another author. People are busy with their lives and won't notice unless you hook their attention with something that is relevant and interesting or entertaining. So if you want to get media attention, you have to find ways to make you and your book newsworthy.

You have to find the story within the story, and that will either be about your personal life or aspects of your book, whether it's fiction or non-fiction.

Go through your life and your influences. What are the consistent themes?

Brainstorm a list and how they might connect to news items, as well as what media they could feature in. For non-fiction, it's pretty easy to find the hooks in your book, but make sure you look for the stories behind that. Use research to craft a story, or use a particular anecdote or hook into a story that is current.

For example, I made it onto national TV in Australia as part of a feature about the best job in the world, caretaker of an island on the Great Barrier Reef, a campaign run by Tourism Queensland that went viral a few years back. The piece featured me as an expert on career change, so even if you didn't get the dream job as island caretaker, you could find something better than your current position.

For fiction, you often need to think tangentially. For example, I was featured in a Forbes article on why many female authors use initials to ensure that gender is not an issue for male readers. The article mentions my *ARKANE* series but is essentially a gender politics piece about publishing and is more about me as the author.

Pick out themes from your book

My ARKANE thrillers have aspects of religion, psychology and international travel with scenes set all over the world. A psychology magazine interviewed me about dreams and the influence of Carl Jung on my fiction. A niche publication for sure, but a fantastic hook into my work, especially as *Stone of Fire* features Jung's Red Book.

Author Polly Courtney writes commercial fiction about big themes in society, including how women fare in the City of London, and the experience of young people during the London riots. Polly hooked into those themes, appearing on TV to discuss related news items. She also used her own story as an author to get press, when she split with her traditional publisher over the covers being "too chick-lit."

Decide on your boundaries

I once had a session with a publicist to discuss doing some PR around my author brand. Within a few minutes of starting the conversation, she asked questions about the failure of my first marriage, how much money I earned, why I didn't have children, and other personal questions that had nothing to do with my books. "People want to know about you, not the book," she said. "We need to find interesting hooks for a story, and personal things are the most interesting."

After that call, I decided not to go any further. I like sharing my pictures on Twitter, Instagram and Facebook, and I'm happy to write articles on my own site because I control the message. I write the words and choose the pictures, and I edit them to keep a part of my life private. If you decide to open up to the media, then you no longer control what might get out there.

Yes, there is an up-side, but there may also be scrutiny over your private life.

The media will choose the soundbites and spin the story how they want. You don't get to edit or choose the parts that portray you in the best light. You don't get to pick the headline or the angle for the story. If you are featured, be generous with your information, but don't be naive. It's not the journalist's job to make you look good, and they will use whatever angle works best to attract attention.

I was once quoted out of context in a mainstream national UK newspaper and made out to be something I'm not by someone who took offense at me. The quote came from a public speaking event I did, so I didn't even know there would be media reporting on it. I was upset and offended, but I learned my lesson.

If you do get negative press, don't react publicly.

I got a lot of emails at the time pointing me to the article but I didn't fuel the fire by joining in. Lots of other authors sprang to my defense, but I didn't get involved. Hyping it even further would have just given it more airtime. A few days later, I posted a reasoned article on my site explaining my stance in detail. Unsurprisingly, that piece got no attention, because, at the end of the day, people are far more interested in the snarky opinion pieces! So, be aware of what you say and how you behave at all times.

> "I would advise anyone who aspires to a writing career that before developing his talent he would be wise to develop a thick hide."
>
> *Harper Lee*

Create a compelling press release or media pitch

Think of the press release as a story hook sent to the right person at the right time. It might also be a story pitch, rather than a specific piece of news.

Back when I focused on targeting traditional media, I sent a press release just before Christmas to ten hand-picked journalists. It included an article titled "Top 10 Career Related New Year's Resolutions" that they could use in full or copy and paste quotes from. Lists and top tips are popular with sites as they offer value for the reader and are not too long. I included information about my book, *Career Change.*

That one press release resulted in an article in the print and online edition of the local paper, a blog post on *Mindfood,* a women's magazine similar to *Psychologies,* an article in *MX,* a free commuter newspaper distributed on public transport in major metropolitan areas, a national radio interview, and a segment on a national TV news program, Channel 9's *A Current Affair.* This was back when I lived in Australia, but the principles hold true wherever you live.

I had sent out press releases before and had no response,

but this worked because I targeted my audience, sending specifically addressed emails to named individuals. I sent the press release at a 'dead news' time – just before Christmas – so journalists working over the holiday would have something to use, plus it was a positive story, which is great at that time of year. Being helpful to journalists means they have less work to do. I was available immediately for interviews and photos and made room in my schedule for TV and radio.

In retrospect, it could have been even better if I had followed up with other journalists who didn't respond and tried to level up that initial success into other opportunities on bigger news outlets. However, this takes time, energy and focus that I didn't have, as I was still working full-time at that point. I would probably have benefited from media training as I was nervous. But after that first time, it was much easier, and when I made it onto Sky News, BBC News and Asian network Zee TV a few years later, I was much more relaxed.

Tips for press releases

Identify what you want to say and who your target is. Tailor the release to the individual, otherwise it will be rejected immediately. Preferably use the name of the appropriate journalist and know what they usually write about.

Monitor media feeds. If you respond quickly, professionally and with information that helps a journalist write a story to deadline, you can get into the media quite easily. Check out HelpAReporter.com or #journorequest on Twitter.

You can write a pitch or press release anytime. The launch of your book may not be as newsworthy as an article you write that is timely and interesting. Keep an eye on the news for topics that relate to your books over time, then target journalists with comments and facts about that situation.

Keep your pitch short, around 500-800 words, so it can be scanned quickly. If you email, don't include an attachment as it will likely get stuck in spam. Just put the press release in the body of the email. You can send it physically in the post with something that makes it stand out but be aware that many of these end up in the trash unless they really are special.

Make it a story that features you, not an advert for your book. **Use a quote** from someone, or yourself to make the point stand out. Remember to include **your contact details** and website links.

Focus on the outcome. Consider what you want people to do after the story, for example, go to your website and sign up or buy your book.

Respond to media requests quickly, or the journalist will find someone else. They are usually working to a deadline.

For more detail, I recommend *Your Press Release is Breaking my Heart: A Totally Unconventional Guide to Selling Your Story in the Media* by Janet Murray. You can also listen to an interview with Janet at:

www.TheCreativePenn.com/janet

4.24 Tips for TV and radio

Authors are frequently on TV or radio as experts on particular topics, and if you focus on marketing, you will likely end up in the traditional media at some point. It's just part of life as an author, so you might as well be prepared. Here are some tips based on my experiences.

Before the interview

If you do get a call to be on TV or radio, the journalist or station liaison will arrange the details on when you need to be there. They may send a car for you, or you might meet them on location.

Do your research beforehand.

Get to know the station and host in advance, listen or watch the show and get a sense of the interviewer's style and personal bias? Google the host to find out more about them. LinkedIn and Twitter are great for finding out more on journalists these days, so you can build rapport quickly when you arrive.

If you're doing a piece for TV, they may want you to pose with props, so take along anything that might be useful and make sure you bring your print books, just in case. They may also want you to do specific activities while they film and you may have to do these multiple times until the shots are complete. In 2014, Amazon made a short film about my author journey and the four minutes took nearly eight hours to put together, filming shots multiple times. You can watch it at:

www.TheCreativePenn.com/amazonvideo

If you're feeling anxious or nervous beforehand, then don't worry, that's completely normal. I felt physically sick before my first TV appearance and even now, I get heart palpitations and sweats before doing a podcast or radio interview. But I've found that the **anticipation is often worse than the actual event.**

You might build something up in your head, but it ends up being a casual chat with someone who (generally) wants to make you look good. Unless of course, you're writing deliberately controversial material and you're spoiling for a fight!

If the interview is live, **try to arrange a recording.** Many stations will have playback snippets later, but they disappear over time, so it's good to have your own version as backup.

Make sure you're early or on time. When you arrive, there may or may not be someone to help with makeup if you're on TV, so be sure to have whatever you need with you. It might also be useful to bring some different outfits just in case, as I had one experience where my (professional looking) dress was considered too short for a particular cultural audience, and I had to sit with it pulled down awkwardly over my knees during the show.

During the interview

The studio is likely to be empty apart from you and the journalist. This surprised me the first time I was on TV, but it should help you relax. Just think of it as just a casual chat. A technician will help you with sound, and it's important to ask any questions before the interview starts. Don't be afraid to ask as the team will be used to questions and will want to put you at ease. Try to get some pictures of yourself at this point if there's time. Photos in the studio are great for social media!

If you're phoning into a radio show, have everything nearby but don't rustle or crackle. Shuffling paper sounds terrible on the radio, so if you're doing a phone interview, lay your notes around you so you can glance at them if necessary. But aim to be prepared enough that you don't need to rely on notes. Always have a glass of water handy, especially if it's a long interview.

When you're being interviewed, look at the journalist or presenter, not the camera. **Be engaging but don't push your book.** You are being featured as an expert opinion, not as a salesperson. It's about contributing to the story that the journalist is trying to tell so make them look good. Assume that they haven't read your book and help them rather than trying to catch them out. Focus on being interesting and lively, and the host will (hopefully) mention your book title and website.

If you're worried about your looks or your voice, get over yourself! No one is interested in you, they're interested in how you can entertain or help *them*. So focus on pleasing your audience and just get on with it.

Smile, even if you are on the phone because your enthusiasm can be heard in your voice. If you're on audio only, then I recommend standing up because that also gives your voice more energy. I have a standing-sitting desk and always stand for any audio recording whether it's my podcast or an interview on another show.

If you are useful and professional, they might consider calling you again next time they need an expert on the topic.

Take some deep breaths. I was nervous right up to the point of being introduced on my first radio show. My mouth was dry, and I needed the bathroom for the fifth time. My heart was racing. But once the host said, "welcome to the show," I was fine. So, take some deep breaths before being introduced and try to have fun! If you know your topic, you'll be fine.

Be prepared for success. Make sure your website is ready, and your contact details are up to date, just in case you do get a spike in traffic and sales.

After the interview

Update your website and media kit with 'as seen on' details about your appearance. You can also use it as a way to get more exposure by immediately pitching the story to related journalists where you can mention where you've been featured.

Say yes to everything appropriate. Even if you get no extra sales from your book, you never know who might be listening and what may happen next, or where that one connection might lead. There are stories of authors being on late night shows for tiny stations, only to find the segment syndicated across the country. If you can get radio time or a podcast interview, then take those opportunities!

This section of the book has been all about the long-term marketing tactics that you can put in place to grow your readership and book sales over the years of your author career. In the next section, we'll focus specifically on marketing strategy and book launches.

Part 5: Marketing Strategy and Book Launches

5.1 Your book marketing strategy

Strategy is deciding what you want to do, and perhaps more importantly, what you *don't* want to do.

That second part is really important, and something many authors lose sight of. If you try to do everything in this book, you will end up burned out, frustrated and exhausted, wondering why the hell you're bothering.

What's your why?

You also need to determine *why* you're putting all this effort into marketing, and this comes back to your definition of success as discussed at the beginning of this book. I'll assume if you've made it this far that you want to sell some books, make some money and perhaps even be an author for the long term. But it's definitely worth writing down your why, so you can look at it when you feel like it's all a bit much!

I love creating new things in the world. I love writing and producing books, educating, inspiring and entertaining people with my words. I write to help people, but also to work out what I think about life. I'm a full-time author entrepreneur, and I also write to earn a (very good) living. Marketing is an important part of my business because it's about reaching readers who might be interested in my books.

There are two aspects to your book marketing strategy – your launch or relaunch, otherwise known as spike marketing, and then what you will put in place for the long term. You will need to consider each type for your brand or author name.

It's important to think beyond just a launch, because once you've got the book off the ground, you want to keep sales ticking on and it's easier to do that with a little constant care. It takes a lot of effort and fuel to get an aircraft off the ground, but once it's airborne, you just need to keep it flying. Maintaining momentum is much easier than getting things started.

You also need to make sure that you stay focused, because scattergun marketing is not as effective. So choose, focus, put your marketing plan into action and then review later when you can decide on what you've learned and what to change. Don't get distracted by shiny object syndrome.

How do you manage your strategy?

Some authors love to create a detailed spreadsheet or project management template that includes all their marketing activities, with specific dates and activities marked out. Others will just wing it. I'm somewhere in between!

Wherever you sit on the spectrum, it's worth having some kind of plan. It will change over time, and it will be different per book. I have three main author brands, and they all have different marketing practices associated with them. Here's my marketing strategy for each, with the assumption that your genre-specific book cover, sales description, categories and keywords are all in place.

Joanna Penn. Non-fiction books, courses and professional speaking

For on-going long-term marketing:

- Permafree book on all ebook stores: *Successful Self-Publishing*, that leads people to my other books as well as back to my website for tutorials and affiliate links

- Author 2.0 Blueprint. Free ebook and video series as my list-builder and a 15 email auto-responder sequence that includes tutorials and useful information at www.TheCreativePenn.com/blueprint

- Monthly newsletter with personal photos, useful articles and thoughts on writing

- Weekly audio podcast

- Weekly YouTube video

- Bi-weekly blog posts with search engine optimized headlines aimed at my target market of authors and writers

- Speaking and live events several times a year

- Daily Twitter and Facebook updates

- Guest interviews on other targeted podcasts around writing, creativity, and entrepreneurship

- Regular print book giveaways on Goodreads

For spike marketing:

- Use of pre-orders for new ebooks

- Email to my non-fiction list

- Podcast announcement
- Facebook and Amazon Ads for books, audiobooks, webinars and events

J.F.Penn. Thrillers

For on-going long-term marketing:

- Writing in series which gathers readers over time
- First book in my main series free on all ebook stores
- Free thriller giveaway to build my email list at JFPenn.com/free
- PennFriends Street Team for early reviews
- Use of box-sets and price promotions on all stores
- Co-writing with other authors
- Amazon Ads for similar authors
- Bi-monthly articles on interesting topics on JFPenn. com
- Facebook updates several times a week
- Occasional Instagram pictures
- A Board per book on Pinterest
- Regular print book giveaways on Goodreads

For spike marketing:

- Price promotions on free books or reduced boxsets
- Paid email blasts like BookBub, BargainBooksy and others

- Facebook advertising to my list, LookaLike audiences and targeting other authors

- Participation in Bundles and cross-promoting with other genre authors

- Application for promotions on Kobo and Apple Books

Secret sweet romance / contemporary women's fiction author

This is a new pen-name for me at the time of writing and in order to keep the readers specifically targeted, I haven't shared it with my wider audience. So, I'm essentially starting again with no platform and no email list.

It's also not a brand I will be actively managing on social media and I won't be doing content marketing either. The marketing needs to be as passive as possible, so it is largely based around book-specific marketing and paid ads.

For on-going long-term marketing:

- Writing in a series with each book leading into another

- Use of KDP Select for the added visibility and voracious market

- Amazon Ads on sweet romance authors

- Basic author website with email sign-up to build list over time

- Facebook page with one scheduled picture per day, mainly so that the Page can be used for advertising

- Regular print book giveaways on Goodreads

For spike marketing:

- Facebook Ads on targeted sweet romance authors

- KDP Select free days and paid promotion to get traffic to the book on those days

- BookBub and other paid email promotion

You can see that there are different combinations of long-term marketing and spike marketing for each of my author brands. It might seem like a lot to do, but once you get things set up, many of these activities are easily managed. There are ongoing marketing activities for each brand, but I also have a specific focus per month, so each brand gets four months per year when I push it even further.

You will find every author has a different marketing strategy based on the genre they write and what kind of person they are. Your list will look different again.

5.2 Aspects of a book launch

"Marketing is figuring out who wants to buy what you're selling, then making sure they're aware it exists."

Chris Fox, *Launch to Market*

People often get hung up on the book launch for marketing. A launch *can* be important, but most of this book is about long-term marketing that you can do for your entire career. After all, it's far better to sell millions of books over the long term than get hung up on a few thousand over launch week.

The launch period is mainly about overcoming the inertia of a new book with no sales history, as well as trying to hit bestseller lists if that's appropriate. But the real sales are likely to happen over time, so don't be disappointed if your launch results are lower than expected. It may be that a relaunch when your next book comes out is more effective, because a book is new to the reader who has just found it anyway. You get to choose what you do for your book.

Even if your book is traditionally published, you can work alongside the assigned publicist to make the launch even better.

Why the obsession with book launches?

Traditionally, publishers have focused on their front-list titles, books they market hard on launch before they move onto the next book. The turnover in a bookstore is usually 4-6 weeks, or 8-12 weeks for hardback. That's not very long to grab an audience and get them to buy. The publisher may even pulp the books that aren't sold in this period, or bulk sell them as remainders, so the initial launch period has always been critical for success.

But now we have unlimited shelf space with online stores. New readers can discover your books every day. They can buy the ebook, audiobook or print book online and there's no out-of-print and no pulping with print-on-demand. The books are always available, so you don't have to go into scarcity mode and try to sell them all in the first two weeks. You can cultivate an abundance mentality where everyone you connect with can buy your books, whenever they hear about you. Every sale goes into the algorithms and creates on-going sustainability with a long-term payoff.

Of course, it's still a good idea to do some launch activities to get your book moving. Here are some elements that you could consider.

3 - 6 months before launch

Decide on your definition of success and your budget in terms of time and money.

You have to decide what you want for your launch and the costs and benefits of each option, as well as what you're willing to give in terms of time and money. For example, you could hire a video production team and pay for TV advertising across the whole of the US, as James Patterson did for his launch of *Along Came A Spider* when he first started out.

Or you could write some guest blog posts and schedule an online book launch party with giveaways, plus use Facebook ads to reach readers of similar books. This will cost a lot less money and (most likely) be a lot more effective than TV ads these days.

If you're self-publishing, you need to choose whether you will go exclusive with KDP Select, because that will impact where to focus your launch.

Plan your dates.

If you're traditionally published, you won't have much choice on your book launch period, but if you're self-published, you get to determine your dates. Although the book will become available to buy on one particular day, you should plan on several weeks of focused promotion to allow for momentum in the charts.

Reserve your slots for guest blogging, interviews, blog book tours, or anything else you're arranging with other sites. If you're working with a publicist, help them organize media opportunities as well as booking advertising slots and paid reviews like Publishers Weekly.

Block out your schedule so that you have time to do all the promotion, and get enough rest. Pretty much every author I know gets exhausted at launch time!

Build relationships with authors and influencers in your niche.

If you start commenting or tweeting or sharing other people's books or content, you can start to build a relationship with them over time. This goes back to social karma, but basically, you are far more likely to get a guest blog spot or podcast interview or email to their list if you build a relationship before pitching. Start by networking with your own peer group and then build up to connecting with influencers if you can.

Build your email list and your Street Team.

Even if you're just starting out, chances are this won't be your last book! Your list will start small, but over time, you can build it up and then you can ask a sub-set to join your Street Team as covered in chapter 4.7.

Sort out your book fundamentals.

These include the cover, sales description, keywords and categories, as well as understanding the target market for your book. You will need all these elements for your launch and on-going marketing, and they are critical for success.

Set up pre-orders if appropriate.

Pre-orders are available on all the ebook stores and can also be done for print books through Ingram Spark. You can set them up to 90 days in advance on Amazon and up to a year on Apple Books and Kobo, even if you don't have a cover.

The benefits of pre-orders include the ability to start marketing early, get double sales ranking on Apple Books, which counts sales before and after launch, visibility on lists on Amazon, Kobo and other sites, and early population of also-boughts. It also means you can get everything organized before your launch, which can help if you have a lot of other activities organized. Authors who choose to publish wide will often have pre-orders on Apple Books, Kobo and Nook months in advance but will only set one up on Amazon a few days before in order to concentrate the ranking there.

It's not worth using pre-orders if you're putting out your first book or have a very small audience, but it can be useful for later books in a series, or if you already have an audience waiting for your work.

One month before launch

Set up your book page and links on your author website with pre-order links if appropriate

Send out your Advanced Reader Copies with the dates that you will need the reviews.

Prepare and send any **guest articles** or marketing material you promised to other bloggers, authors or reviewers, so it is all done in advance

Prepare or commission any **promotional images** or advertising that you need

One week before 'official' launch

It's a good idea to do a **soft launch** in order to sort out your metadata and get initial reviews, before telling the wider world that your book is available. This is harder if you have set up pre-orders, but it's worth scheduling any promotional spike activities for at least a week after the book is on sale to make sure everything is working correctly. This is especially useful if you are new to self-publishing, because you're not used to the way things work, and it takes a few hours for changes to go through.

Add your links to your book page and Goodreads and any other sites like BookBub. I use BookLinker.net to create a global URL for Amazon that includes my affiliate tags, but you can also set up a universal link at www.books2read.com

Claim your book through Amazon Author Central, so it is linked to your author name

Reformat or tweak your sales description to make it look good and add any extra metadata. Check your pricing and the Look Inside.

Buy your book so you can check for any issues with interior formatting. You can always upload a new version if there are problems.

Email your Street Team or early reviewers and remind them to add early reviews.

On launch day

Drive readers to your book sales page. This might include:

- Emailing your list with buy links

- Using Facebook ads, Amazon ads or other paid advertising

- Scheduling a promotion on email blast sites

- Adding images and quotes on social media

- Collaborating with other authors for co-promotion on social media, competitions, giveaways or email lists

- Doing podcasts and guest posts around your book. This is still very effective for non-fiction in particular.

- PR and media appearances

- Live events and speaking

Basically, anything that we've covered in this book or anything else you can think of that will get your book some attention when it goes live.

You can also encourage your audience to buy in launch week by offering **a lower price or bonuses for a limited time.** Building your list is the best way to control sales to readers who love your work. Offering it to them at a lower price for an initial period is both a reward for supporting you and a way to ensure sales in a specific period. For example, a full-price novel at $4.99 could launch to your list at 99c for three days before you raise the price.

Have a book launch party or event.

Many authors dream of the book launch party: Champagne, toasts to the literary genius and crowds of eager readers buying hundreds of books. But in reality, the book launch party is more about rewarding yourself for a job well done, a celebration of a goal achieved, rather than a way of marketing and selling your book.

If you're going to have one, then fantastic! Make sure your friends come along and have a great time, sign some books and enjoy yourself. Take lots of pictures and share them on social media. Maybe even hire a pro photographer to make sure you get some good shots to use in your marketing, but understand that the launch party is not a book marketing technique, but more of a fun time to celebrate.

I've never had a physical book launch party, but one day when I have written more books and achieved my own definition of success, I intend to have more of an author career celebration when I will spend some serious money and have a serious party. Bring it on!

You could also put on a useful or entertaining event that just happens to have a book launch incorporated.

Non-fiction author Trevor Young did a social media strategy event for entrepreneurs featuring a panel of well-known bloggers giving valuable advice. As part of the evening, Trevor also launched his book, *MicroDomination*. People came for the event but left with a copy of his new book.

A physical launch event is location-specific and will only impact sales locally. But these days we can sell to a global audience, so doing an online launch is likely to generate more sales. Some authors have virtual launch parties on Facebook and invite their readers, offering giveaways and gift cards. They spend several hours chatting with fans, creating a party atmosphere that people can join virtually from all over the world.

Online marketing launch activities like articles, interviews, podcasts, and videos will stay online for the long term, so they provide long-tail traffic and hopefully sales into the future.

Take screen prints of your chart position.

I have pictures of my books next to Lee Child, Stephen King, James Patterson and other big-name authors that look great as social proof. If you have published direct on platforms like KDP and Kobo, you'll also be able to watch the sales figures spike, although remember that it can take a few hours to kick in.

After the launch

Thank everyone who was involved, including your readers, bloggers and reviewers. Foster those relationships for next time and make sure that you try to help other people out with their launches too.

Write down anything that was particularly effective and anything that was a waste of time or energy. Reflect on your definition of success and what you can learn from the experience, then put some of your long-term marketing activities into place, so your sales continue over time.

Remember, there are many different ways to launch

Earlier this year, a British author had an exclusive launch party on the Grand Canal in Venice, paid for by her publisher. She was in the national press, sold a lot of books and hit the bestseller lists. But that's not the reality of most book launches for most authors.

When I launch a new book, I set up pre-orders, get early reviews from my Street Team, do an email blast and run paid ads over launch week. I focus a lot more on continuous long-term marketing and spike sales of older books than I do on launching new ones.

So make an effort during your launch, but remember, it's just the start of your book marketing journey.

5.3 Relaunching older books

New authors often have huge expectations around hitting bestseller lists and selling millions of copies on launch. The reality is often quite different.

But the good news is that your book is a long-term investment, and it should be bringing you income for years to come.

It's never too late to market your book, and it will be new for the reader who discovers it today, even if it came out years ago.

Would you rather make $1000 in one week and then never make another cent? Or would you rather make $100 a month for the next five years, giving you a total of $6000?

You'll rank better in launch week if you choose the former, but you'll have more of a chance to make a living as a writer if you aim for the latter. Of course, both would be nice!

Here are some ideas if you want to relaunch or rejuvenate your backlist titles in order to kickstart your sales again.

Change your cover.

This is a tactic that traditional publishers use all the time. The older classics have been through multiple cover redesigns over the years as an excuse to market the books again. I've changed covers and even titles as a way to reposition my books. Indie authors can easily upload new covers or interior files for the book. Revisit the bestselling books in your target categories and commission new designs based on what is working right now.

Redo your metadata.

Before you drive traffic to your book sales page, it's best to optimize your metadata first. Revisit your categories and keywords, because more granular categories are added all the time. For example, literary fiction used to be one category and now has multiple levels below that, and you will rank better and be more discoverable in a more granular category. Check your author page – is it up to date? You could even redo your sales description to take advantage of copywriting best practices.

Schedule a price promotion.

The promotional sites like BookBub often need a significant number of reviews, so they are best to apply for months or even years after initial launch. You can schedule multiple promotions as I did with the ARKANE boxset five years after launch in chapter 3.6.

Pick a newsworthy story or event.

You can relaunch or re-market on a specific day or when a relevant newsworthy topic hits the headlines. For example, if you have a historical book around a place or person, look for anniversaries or events you can hook into. Many romance authors relaunch Christmas-themed books every year, joining with other authors to do giveaways or boxsets.

* * *

Essentially, you can do any of the marketing activities in this book for an older backlist title, and in fact, it is likely to be more effective than an initial launch because your book will have more reviews and you will have more of a clue what you're doing.

My book marketing knowledge improves every year, and I am always adding new things into the mix. The more books I have, the easier they are to market, and I often focus on pushing older books because they have more social proof.

So, the launch mentality can be useful for the short term, but overall, **focus on a long-term, brand-building approach that pays off in sales and relationships over time.** After all, we're in this for the long haul!

Conclusion and next steps

Being a writer is a long-term game, and so is marketing your books. You don't have to do everything, and in fact, you'd be mad to try it all, but over your career, you will likely try pieces from each section.

It will take some time for you to find what marketing works best for your book and for your personality, but that's OK. There is no limited shelf life for your book and there's no rush to sell tons of books on launch anymore. You can learn and implement over time. That's certainly what I've done in the ten years since I started writing, back in the days when I knew nothing about marketing.

In saying that, it's easy to get overwhelmed by the sheer volume of options, so let's just go through the non-negotiables.

(1) **Make sure that your book is the best it can be** and I recommend professional editing and professional cover design to achieve this. All the marketing in the world won't sell a crappy book.

(2) **Identify your comparison books and authors**, because this is the best way to ensure you have a genre-specific cover as well as the right categories and it will help you with so many other marketing activities.

(3) **Optimize your book sales page** with a great sales description, targeted categories, keywords, and optimum pricing. Then get some reviews on your book. You can do this by using free promotions if you don't have an email list.

(4) If you have even a small budget, use **paid promotion** to send readers to your book page, boosting sales or paid reads as well as ensuring you get reviews over time.

(5) If you intend to write more books, set up a professional looking **website** and an **email list sign-up.** Start building your list for the next book now so that you are in a more confident position next time around.

Look into everything else when you have these basics sorted.

If you're already off and running with blogging or social, then no worries. Just check that you have the basics in place before you go any further.

Now take a deep breath and let's revisit the marketing mindset. Because there are so many tactics and tools and tips out there that some authors get overwhelmed and give up completely. But if you have a positive attitude and the willingness to learn, you can build your marketing skills for the long-term. I hope this book has empowered you to get started.

So what are you waiting for? Go market your book!

Need more help?

The book marketing landscape continues to change , so if you'd like to stay up to date, join my reader list and you'll get the **free Author 2.0 Blueprint** ebook and video series, plus info-packed newsletters. Sign up at:

www.TheCreativePenn.com/blueprint

I also report on my weekly podcast.
Check out The Creative Penn podcast on iTunes, Stitcher and other services.

* **

If you found this book useful,
I'd really appreciate a short review.

Your help in spreading the word is gratefully appreciated and reviews make a huge difference to helping new readers find the books.

Thank you and happy book marketing!

Appendix 1: Questions to answer honestly if your book isn't selling

If your book isn't selling what you hoped it would, then use these questions as a checklist to determine whether you've done everything possible to help it reach the right readers.

Of course, you don't have to do everything on this list, but choosing elements from each section will help your book stand out from the crowded market. If you want to fill it in, you can download it at:

www.TheCreativePenn.com/marketingquestions

Marketing principles

- Do you have the right attitude and mindset toward marketing? Have you reframed it as a positive, creative process that can be incorporated into your author life?

- Are you taking responsibility for your book sales success? Or are you waiting for others to do the work for you?

- Are you willing to learn new things and give marketing ideas a try?

- Do you understand that marketing is more than just a book launch?

- Have you set aside a budget in terms of time and/or money for your book marketing?

- Have you decided on the WHY behind your book marketing? What drives you? What will keep you going through difficult times?

- Have you decided on your definition of success for this book and for the next five years of your author career?

- Have you identified where you sit on the various polarities of marketing?

- Have you worked out how to schedule time for writing and marketing activities within your busy life?

- Have you looked into using a Virtual Assistant to help you with marketing if you're struggling on your own?

- What kind of marketing is fun and sustainable for you? What is the best use of your time and resources?

- What have you learned from your book marketing activities in the last 30 days? How can you use your lessons learned to improve your marketing for the next 30 days?

- Have you decided how you will cope when it all becomes too much and you get overwhelmed?

Your book fundamentals

- Are you happy that you have produced the best book you can for the readers you want to reach?

- Have you identified your comparison authors?

- Have you clearly identified your target market? Do you know where they hang out online or offline and where you could reach them?

- Is your cover design professional and suitable for the categories you are publishing in? Does it resonate with your genre and give the reader clear expectations for the book?

- Have you read through and noted down the elements of the sales descriptions from bestselling books in your category?

- Have you written and optimized your book sales description based on copywriting principles?

- Have you spent time looking at the categories where your comparison authors sit on the online bookstores? Do you have a list of categories that would suit your book?

- Do you have a list of keywords that you can use in your book's metadata? Have you considered using some of the useful tools to help you choose the best keywords?

- Have you decided on whether you will publish exclusively on Amazon through KDP Select or whether you will go wide? Do you understand the pros and cons of exclusivity? If you have chosen one or the other and you are revisiting older books, have you analyzed your sales by platform and made a decision about changing your publishing process?

- Have you chosen a pricing strategy that suits your situation? Have you checked the prices in your category for similar books? Does your price fit?

- Have you used free or price pulsing along with paid promotion to get your book moving?

- Do you have tiered pricing so readers can try you out for free or cheap and then funnel into your other books?

- Have you considered using boxsets or bundling, whether as a single author or as part of a collaboration?

- Are you writing a series of books or at least aiming for the same type of reader so you can link the books in a boxset? Have you used the Series field when publishing to link the books together on a series page?

- Is your book available as an ebook and a print book? Is it available in all countries on the same day so readers can buy it if they hear about it?

- Have you set up your Amazon Author Central page and linked your book? Have you done this for the UK as well as the US store?

Short-term marketing

- Do you have a notice at the back of your book thanking readers and asking them to leave a review?

- Have you tried using free promotions to get reviews on your book?

- Have you tried using a Goodreads or other giveaways to get reviews on your book?

- Have you identified appropriate book bloggers and review sites and submitted your book to be reviewed?

- Have you sent out Advanced Reader Copies and asked your email list or Street Team to leave reviews?

- Have you identified free or paid promotional services that will email their list or promote on social media? (Remember, BookBub is only one option. There are many more!)

- Have you tried using Amazon Ads?

- Have you tried using Facebook Ads?

- Have you tried using paid advertising on other social media sites or blogs that might be useful for your genre?

- Have you scheduled multiple ads around a particular launch period in order to use the ad stacking method?

- Have you organized your production and release schedule to make the most of the algorithms in the initial 30/60/90 days?

Long-term marketing

- Are you writing more than one book? Are you committed to building a long-term author platform and marketing your books over time?

- Do you have an author platform already? Do you have any way to reach potential readers right now? What can you use from your existing networks?

- What is your promise to the reader? What experience are you offering them? Does your book cover and author brand resonate with that promise?

- Have you decided on your author name? Why might you consider using multiple author names for different books?

- What words, images and colors do you want to be associated with your author brand?

- Revisit your comparison authors. What words, images and colors are associated with their brand

and what can you learn from them? How can you model success?

- Are you using a professional author photo that resonates with your brand?

- Do you understand the principle of co-opetition and social karma? How can you work with other authors in your niche for mutual benefit?

- Have you set up a professional author website that you own with at least an About page, a Book page and a Contact form?

- Do your book pages contain links to all the places your book is sold?

- Have you set up an email list signup and added it to your website?

- Are you offering something of value in exchange for a reader's email on the sign-up page?

- Do you have a notice at the back of your book directing readers to this free offer?

- Have you set up an auto-responder series, even a simple one, for your email list?

- Have you decided what you will send in your regular broadcast emails?

- Are you keeping your list warm by contacting them regularly with useful, entertaining or inspirational content?

- Have you started building a Street Team or review team of super-fan readers?

- Have you decided how you will use content market-ing? How will you use text, video, audio or images in your content marketing schedule?

- Will you maintain a regular blog around your specific niche? How will that tie into your book marketing? What benefits will it provide for your target market? Are you committed for the long term?

- Do you understand the principles of copywriting for headlines and how you can optimize your blog for search engines and traffic?

- Will you pitch for guest blogging on other sites? Have you identified specific target blogs that resonate with your audience? Have you read the submission guide-lines and do you understand what type of content their audience prefer?

- Have you looked at how images are being used in your niche? Have you played with Canva or PicMonkey to create your own images? Have you identified how you will use images as part of your marketing?

- Have you set up social media profiles on the major sites? Have you picked one or two primary social media platforms and linked everything to your author website?

- Do you know what you will share regularly on social media in order to provide value for your target read-ers? Do you understand how social media can sell books?

- Have you spent some time learning how to use the specific social media site/s you want to use? Do you understand the often unspoken rules of social media etiquette?

- Are you being consistent with your social media sharing?

- Are you scheduling your social media to reach readers in different time zones?

- Have you thought about how to optimize your time on social media to avoid time suck? Have you looked at the scheduling tools available?

- Have you considered starting a podcast? If yes, how will that fit into your wider book marketing or business strategy? Do you understand the time it involves and have you budgeted for that?

- Have you listened to podcasts in your niche in order to understand the best way to use podcasting in your book marketing?

- Have you identified and pitched appropriate podcasters in your genre for interviews around your book?

- Have you considered how you could use video in your marketing? Have you watched YouTube and checked view counts to see what type of videos resonate with your audience? Have you tried using live video or video ads to see if that works for your book?

- If you have audiobooks, have you used promo codes to give away copies to audiobook reviewers? Have you promoted your audiobook on podcasts? Have you embedded a SoundCloud clip into your book page? Have you created a separate audio page on your author website? Have you tried paid advertising to audiobook listeners in particular?

- For marketing print books, have you given away ARCs using sites like NetGalley? Have you made sure your book is available at live events or festivals? Have you considered direct mail or advertising to booksellers or libraries? Have you fostered relationships with booksellers or distributors, schools, librarians, book clubs and other places where print books are directly sold?

* Have you considered how merchandizing could fit into your book marketing? Have you checked out print-on-demand merchandizing options at Society 6 and other sites?

* Is there a newsworthy story hook around your book or around you as the author? Have you crafted a press release or story pitch and sent it to targeted journalists?

* Do you understand the pros and cons of seeking out traditional media? If you want to hire a publicist, do you understand how to make that worthwhile?

Launching and relaunching your book

* Have you decided on your book marketing strategy? Do you know what you *will* do and what you *won't* do for this launch or for your author marketing in general?

* Have you focused on one particular book marketing goal so you don't get overwhelmed?

* Do you have a clear idea of what you will action per author name and over what time period?

* If you have already been marketing for a period of time, have you revisited each book and looked at what you could do to relaunch it or improve sales?

- What are your book launch or relaunch dates?

- Have you set aside time in your schedule to focus on your book launch just in case more opportunities come along?

- What is your definition of success for this launch?

- Have you built relationships with influencers or authors in your niche? List them out along with any ideas for working with them on this launch.

- Have you pitched bloggers or podcasters for interviews or guest posts?

- Have you built your email list and told them about the upcoming launch? Have you built a Street Team or do you have early reviewers ready to read?

- If you're using pre-orders, have you set them up on the respective stores?

- Are you ready with your book cover, categories and keywords, as well as your book sales description?

- Have you sent out Advanced Review Copies?

- Have you set up the book page on your website along with links to all respective stores? Have you set up the book page on Goodreads?

- Have you commissioned any images that you will need for marketing?

- Have you pitched a newsworthy idea to journalists or sent out a targeted press release? Are you working with your publicist (if you have one) to ensure maximum reach?

- Have you scheduled price promotions? If you have one major price promotion, have you stacked other ads around that to maximize sales?

- Have you scheduled social media or are you ready to share on launch?

- Have you prepared your book launch party, whether it is physical or digital?

- Have you checked that your book is setup correctly when it's live on the stores? Have you bought it to check the formatting?

- Have you sent out emails and told fans on social media that your book is available?

- Have you taken screen prints of the launch and ranking for social proof later?

- Have you assessed what worked during launch and what you can learn and put into place for next time?

Appendix 2: Useful resources

The following are books, courses, podcasts and tools that I have found useful on the author journey, specifically related to book marketing.

Books

How to Market a Book: Overperform in a Crowded Market - Ricardo Fayet

Discoverability: Help Readers Find You in Today's World of Publishing - Kristine Kathryn Rusch

How to Write a Sizzling Synopsis: A Step-by-Step System for Enticing New Readers, Selling More Fiction and Making your Books Sound Good - Bryan Cohen

Six-Figure Author: Using Data to Sell Books - Chris Fox

Write to Market: Deliver a Book that Sells - Chris Fox

Launch to Market: Easy Marketing for Authors - Chris Fox

Relaunch your Novel: Breathe Life into your Backlist - Chris Fox

Marketing for Writers Who Hate Marketing - James Scott Bell

Your Press Release is Breaking my Heart: A Totally Unconventional Guide to Selling Your Story in the Media - Janet Murray

How to Get Your Self-Published Book into Bookstores - Debbie Young, edited by Orna Ross

The Prosperous Writer's Guide to Finding Readers: Build your Author Brand, Raise your Author Profile, and Find Readers to Delight - Honoree Corder, Brian D. Meeks and Michael Anderle

Merchandising for Authors - Melissa Addey

Unlabel: Selling You Without Selling Out - Marc Ecko

Jab, Jab, Jab, Right Hook - Gary Vaynerchuk

Nobody wants to read your sh*t - Steven Pressfield

Permission Marketing, Purple Cow - and anything else by Seth Godin

Influence: The Psychology of Persuason - Robert Cialdini

To Sell is Human: The Surprising Truth about Moving Others - Daniel H. Pink

Platform: Get Noticed in a Noisy World - Michael Hyatt

Trust Agents: Using the web to build influence, improve reputation and earn trust - Chris Brogan and Julien Smith

Primal Branding: Create Zealots for your Brand, your Company and your Future - Patrick Hanlon

Growth Hacker Marketing - Ryan Holiday

The New Rules of Marketing and PR: How to Use Social Media, Online Video, Mobile Applications, Blogs, News Releases, and Viral Marketing to Reach Buyers Directly - David Meerman Scott

Launch: An Internet Millionaire's Secret Formula to Sell Almost Anything Online, Build a Business you Love, and Live the Life of your Dreams - Jeff Walker

Your First 1000 Copies - Tim Grahl

1001 Ways to Market your Books - John Kremer

Mastering Amazon Ads: An Author's Guide - Brian D. Meeks

Ebook Bundling: Level up your Income with the Power of Bundling - Chuck Heintzelman

Useful podcasts for book marketing

The Sell More Books Show with Bryan Cohen and H. Claire Taylor

The Self-Publishing Show with Mark Dawson and James Blatch

Six Figure Authors with Lindsay Buroker, Andrea Pearson and Joe Lallo

The Creative Penn Podcast with Joanna Penn and guest interviews

Tools

KDP Rocket for analysing keywords:
www.TheCreativePenn.com/rocket

K-lytics for analysing categories:
www.TheCreativePenn.com/genre

ConvertKit for building your email list:
www.TheCreativePenn.com/convert

BookFunnel for delivering free books and ARCs:
www.TheCreativePenn.com/bookfunnel

Reedsy for editors, cover designers and book marketing
professionals: www.TheCreativePenn.com/reedsy

Free tutorials

How to build your own author website in 30 minutes:
www.TheCreativePenn.com/authorwebsite

How to automate your author marketing and build your
first 10,000 readers webinar replay with Nick Stephenson
and Joanna Penn: www.TheCreativePenn.com/nickjo

More tools, tutorials and resources at
www.TheCreativePenn.com/tools

More Books And Courses From Joanna Penn

Non-Fiction Books for Authors

How to Write Non-Fiction

How to Market a Book

How to Make a Living with your Writing

Productivity for Authors

Successful Self-Publishing

Your Author Business Plan

The Successful Author Mindset

Public Speaking for Authors, Creatives
and Other Introverts

Audio for Authors:
Audiobooks, Podcasting, and Voice Technologies

The Healthy Writer

Business for Authors:
How to be an Author Entrepreneur

Co-writing a Book

Career Change

www.TheCreativePenn.com/books

Courses for authors

How to Write a Novel

How to Write Non-Fiction

Multiple Streams of Income from your Writing

Your Author Business Plan

Content Marketing for Fiction

Productivity for Authors

Turn What You Know Into An Online Course

Co-Writing a Book

www.TheCreativePenn.com/courses

Thriller novels as J.F. Penn

ARKANE Action-adventure Thrillers

Stone of Fire #1
Crypt of Bone #2
Ark of Blood #3
One Day In Budapest #4
Day of the Vikings #5
Gates of Hell #6
One Day in New York #7
Destroyer of Worlds #8
End of Days #9
Valley of Dry Bones #10
Tree of Life #11

Brooke and Daniel Crime Thrillers

Desecration #1
Delirium #2
Deviance #3

Mapwalker Dark Fantasy Trilogy

Map of Shadows #1
Map of Plagues #2
Map of the Impossible #3

Other Books and Short Stories

Risen Gods

A Thousand Fiendish Angels:
Short stories based on Dante's Inferno

The Dark Queen:
An Underwater Archaeology Short Story

More books coming soon.

You can sign up to be notified of new releases, giveaways
and pre-release specials - plus, get a free book!

www.JFPenn.com/free

About Joanna Penn

Joanna Penn is a New York Times and USA Today bestselling author of thrillers and dark fantasy under J.F.Penn. She also writes inspirational non-fiction for authors and is an award-winning creative entrepreneur and international professional speaker.

Her site, TheCreativePenn.com is regularly voted one of the top 10 sites for writers and self-publishers. Joanna also has a popular podcast for writers, The Creative Penn.

Joanna has a Master's degree in Theology from the University of Oxford, Mansfield College, and a Graduate Diploma in Psychology from the University of Auckland, New Zealand. She lives in London, England but spent 11 years living in Australia and New Zealand. Joanna enjoys traveling as often as possible. She's obsessed with religion and psychology and loves to read, drink gin and tonic, and soak up European culture through art, architecture and food.

Connect with Joanna online:

www.TheCreativePenn.com/contact
Twitter.com/thecreativepenn
Facebook.com/TheCreativePenn
Youtube.com/thecreativepenn

Joanna also has a popular podcast for writers,
TheCreativePenn.com/podcasts/

Joanna's fiction site: www.JFPenn.com

Acknowledgments

Thanks to all those in the indie author community who generously share their book marketing experience and lessons learned online in blogs, forums and books. Together, we continue to learn, grow and sell more books. It truly is the best time to be an author.

Thanks to Liz Dexter at Libro Editing for line editing, and to Alexandra Amor for beta reading. Thanks to Jane Dixon Smith at JD Smith Design for cover design and interior print formatting.